ABANDONED NEW YORK

CITY OF BROKEN DREAMS

LIZ ROLL

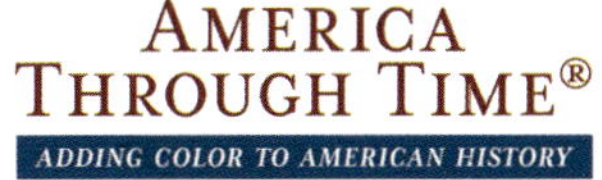

For my mother and father, kindred New Yorkers

America Through Time is an imprint of Fonthill Media LLC
www.through-time.com
office@through-time.com

Published by Arcadia Publishing by arrangement with Fonthill Media LLC
For all general information, please contact Arcadia Publishing:
Telephone: 843-853-2070
Fax: 843-853-0044
E-mail: sales@arcadiapublishing.com
For customer service and orders:
Toll-Free 1-888-313-2665

www.arcadiapublishing.com

First published 2021

ISBN 978-1-63499-300-5

Typeset in Trade Gothic
Printed and bound in England

CONTENTS

ABOUT THE AUTHOR

Liz Roll is a freelance visual solutions provider, storyteller, and photographer in the Washington, D.C./Northern Virginia area. Liz began her career at the American Red Cross as a photographer and eventually moved over to FEMA, the Federal Emergency Management Agency, where she has documented dozens of natural disasters, including Hurricanes Katrina and Sandy. She also does historical documentation (i.e. urban blight) photography, documentary videos, events, conferences, and magazine shoots. Liz photographed many VIPs, including four presidents, three vice presidents, and others too numerous to count. She is an adrenaline junkie.

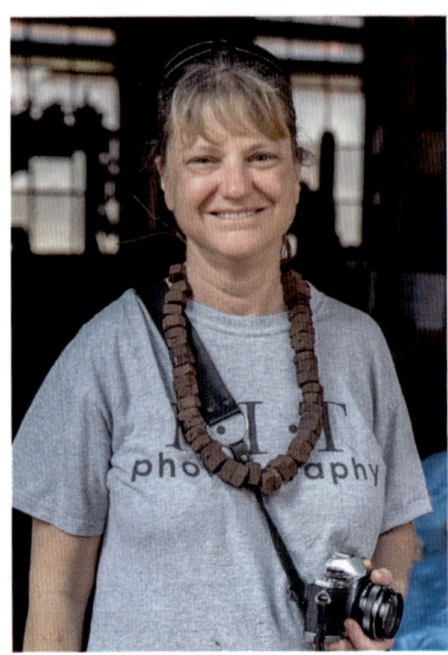

Author Photo by Eric Brown

INTRODUCTION

The Big Apple. Gotham. The City That Never Sleeps. The City of Dreams. Whatever you want to call it, New York City is one of the greatest cities on earth. Every town has its quirky side, and New York is no exception. It is chock-full of abandoned buildings and forgotten hidden gems. Built on a layer of sturdy bedrock, many of the buildings in New York are from the turn of the twentieth century. Imagine seeing a full-size ad for Omega Oil on the side of a building in Harlem. Or train tracks with grass growing up through them, in the middle of Manhattan. Or perhaps an exquisite apartment building, abandoned in Greenwich Village. In New York, abandonments are hard to find, simply because of the shortage of real estate. Sadly, old buildings are quickly converted into condos or repurposed another way. But abandoned buildings do exist—albeit some for only a short period.

While I was growing up near New York, I had the opportunity to go often into Manhattan on the train. I recall seeing Santa on every street corner at Christmas time (my mom telling me they were Santa's "helpers"), taking in the slightly burnt aroma of chestnuts roasting, and the cold nip in the air. I can remember emerging from Penn Station to see trash swirling in the wind like dervishes. I remember the blind nun every year asking for money; I recall the man on the scooter with (apparently) no legs. This was part of the charm of the city, I was not scared and I had no culture shock. The city has cleaned up a lot since then. No longer is 42nd Street feared, one imagining getting yanked against their will into a seedy porn theatre. Now, one could fear being accosted by a Disney character or an nearly-nude Eastern European woman—about as seedy as Times Square gets these days.

Now, I see the city with new eyes. Gotham is clean now, but the grit is missing. It is safe all right, as safe as any big city can be, but sadly, the seediness is gone. To have one, it seems the other must be forfeited.

Abandoned buildings are rare in New York. The history surrounding some of these buildings is astounding—but alas, if they cannot be repurposed, they must go, as real estate is at a premium. Space is limited on that bedrock. Hurry, or you will miss it! I have missed many—Lowes Theatre, The TWA building at JFK, the diner on West River Drive—however, I am pleased that I have photographed what I have. I feel that growing up in New York was the greatest gift my parents afforded me, and for that I am thankful.

1

NO. 5 BEEKMAN STREET

Near the heart of the Financial District, across the street from the Woolworth Building, is a charming little boutique hotel and residences called 5 Beekman. Do not let that fool you—this nine-story building, once known as Temple Court, was abandoned for a long time (eons in New York time), part of it since the 1940s.

An Irish millionaire who immigrated to the United States in the 1800s originally built 5 Beekman as an office building. With Beekman Street's proximity to City Hall and the courts, lawyers occupied many of these offices, although some offices had accountants, insurance agencies, a hospital credit exchange, and other businesses as tenants. The idea of a building with many types of trades was trendsetting at the time, and was just beginning to be in vogue.

The architecture of 5 Beekman should not be overlooked. Built in 1882, Five Beekman is one of very few Manhattan buildings that incorporates a full height atrium and skylight, which is a sight to behold. Five Beekman was the first high-rise building in New York, and it was the third building in New York to have an elevator, which was of the iron cage style. A ten-floor annex was added in 1890. Atop the nine original floors is a pyramid skylight, providing daylight to the interior space. The atrium features the original wrought iron railings and banisters festooned with dragons and sunbursts.

Fireproofing became essential as the buildings in New York got taller. The deadliest fire in New York at the Triangle Shirtwaist Company was still years away (1911), but is an example of why fireproofing became so important. Five Beekman is the earliest surviving example of a fireproof building in New York. Ironically, the atrium and skylight, sealed since the 1940s because the construction violated the newer codes, aided the building's preservation.

Five Beekman was renovated in 2016 into 287 hotel rooms (one night in the hotel will set one back an average of about $300) with residences in the annex section. A new tower was also added. The building features two original turrets, which are now luxury hotel rooms. A lounge is located in the atrium beneath the skylight. Each residence reportedly sold for $1.225 million.

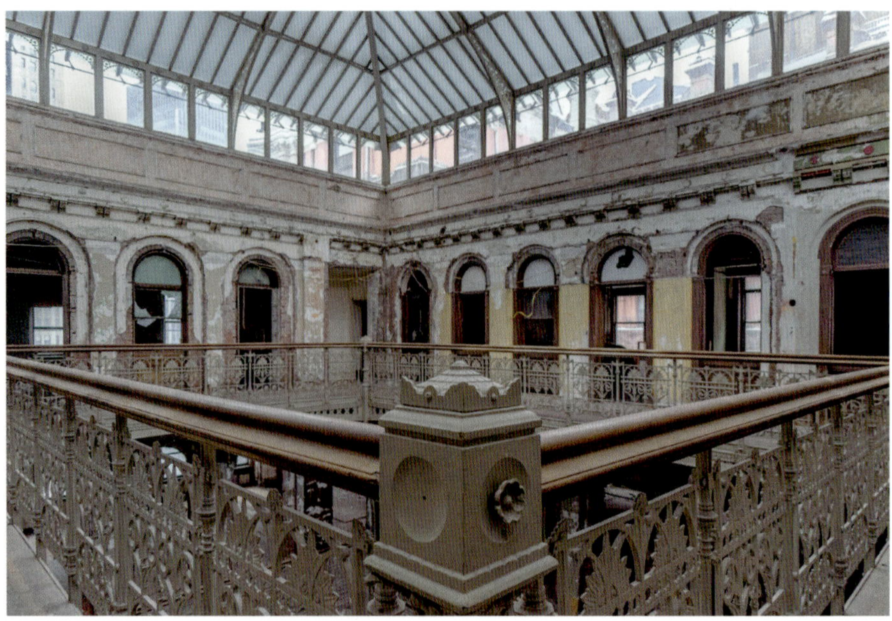

A grand skylight caps the top floor of 5 Beekman (shown here covered by snow). The skylight was only uncovered and restored in the last fifteen or so years.

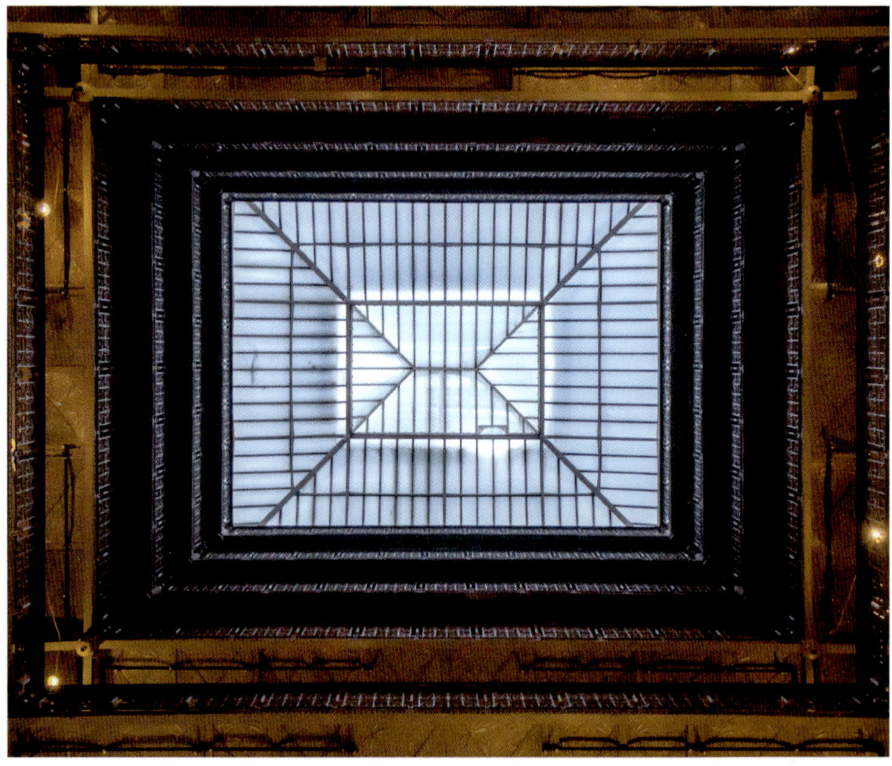

It is a stunning view looking up at the skylight, even with the snow obscuring the view.

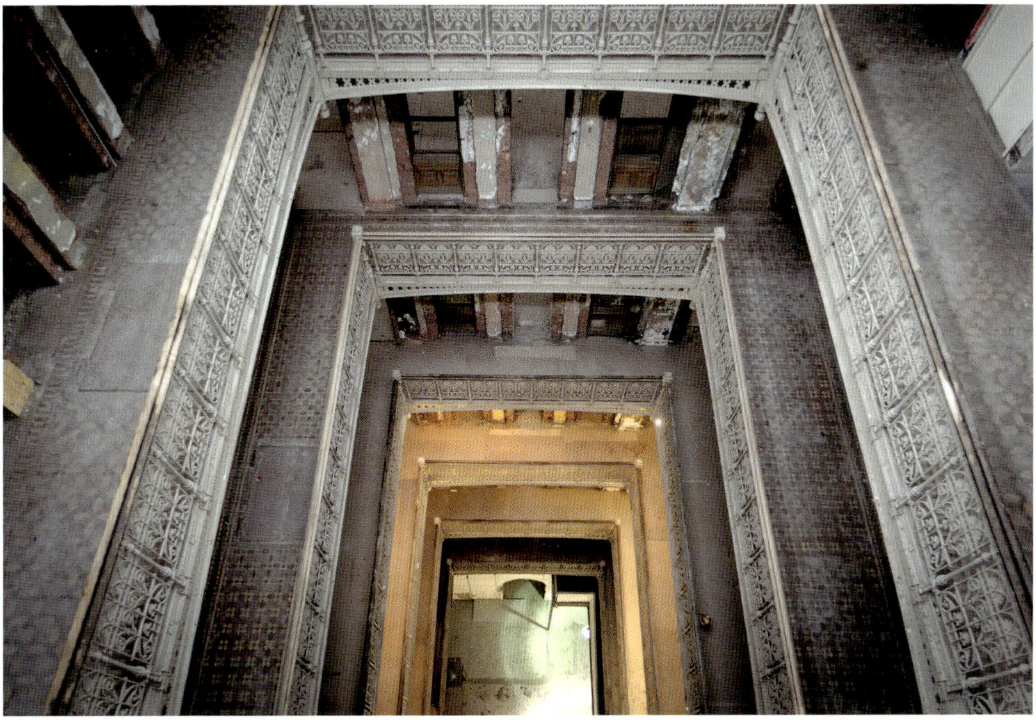

Looking down 5 Beekman's atrium from the sixth floor into an empty lobby, one can see all the intricate ironwork around the balconies.

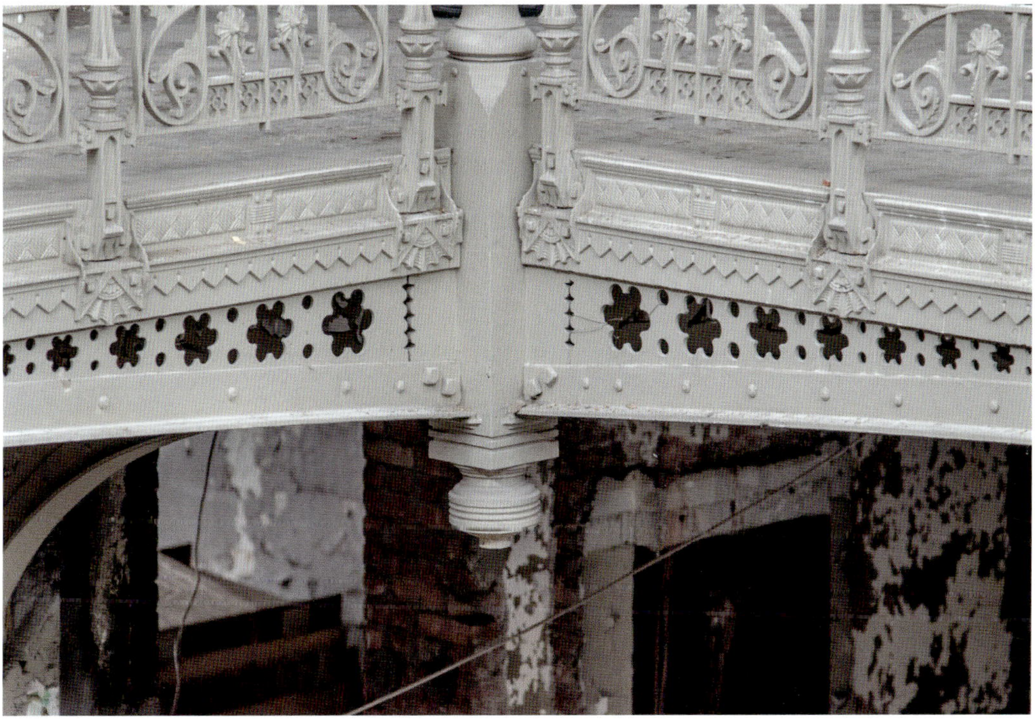

Cast iron supports the floors and the balconies above.

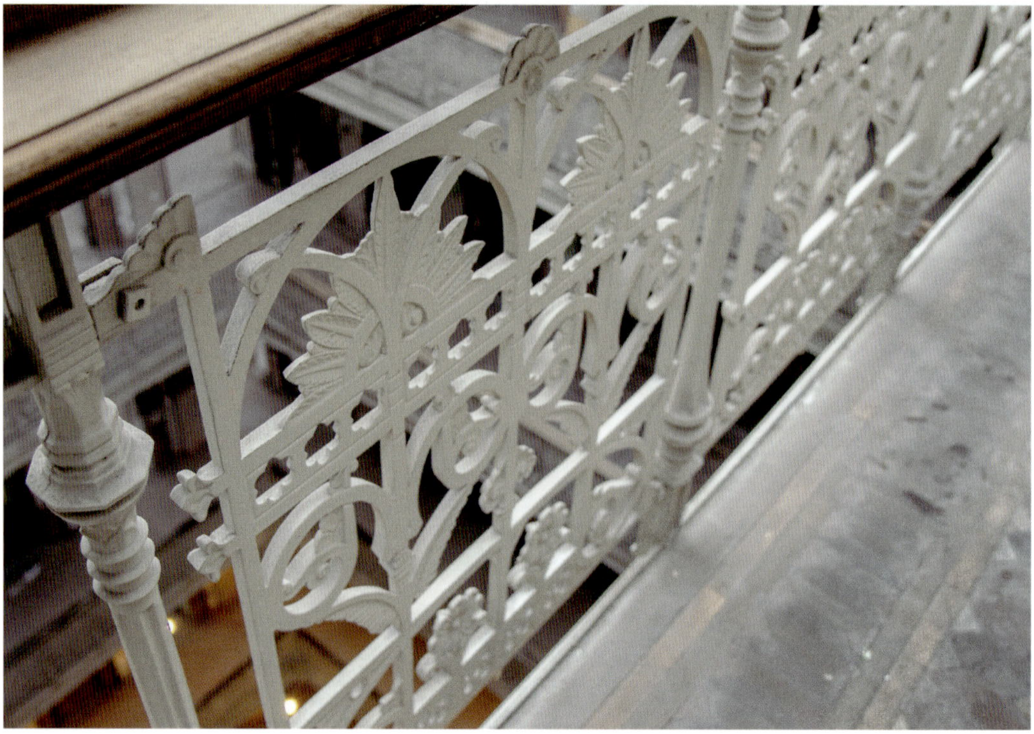

Detail of the ironwork on the balconies; also notice the dusty (but beautiful) inlaid floor.

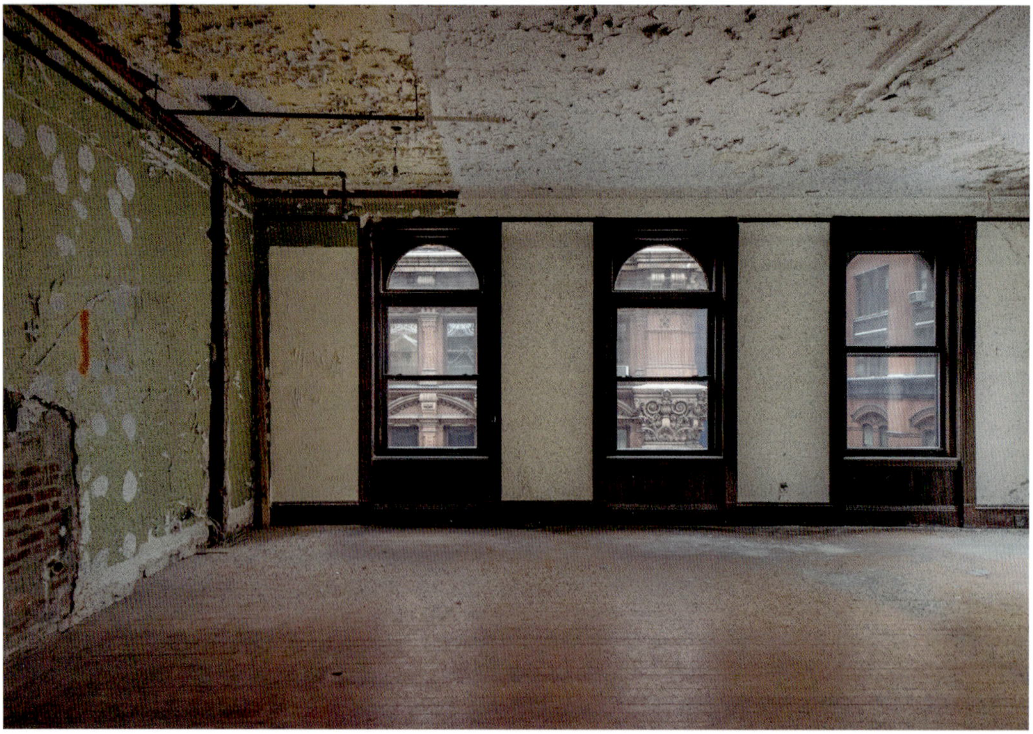

One of the rooms in the upper floors will eventually become one or more hotel rooms.

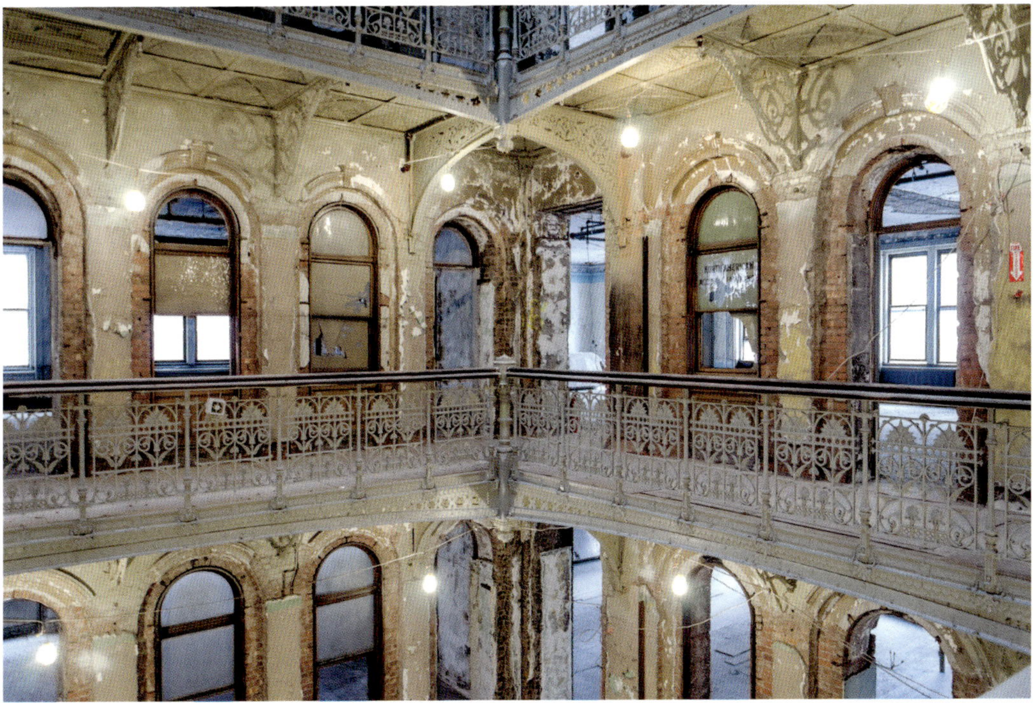

In the window on the middle right, one can make out the remnants of a sign that reads "American Accident Insurance." Also note the elaborate cast-iron dragon brackets holding up the next balcony.

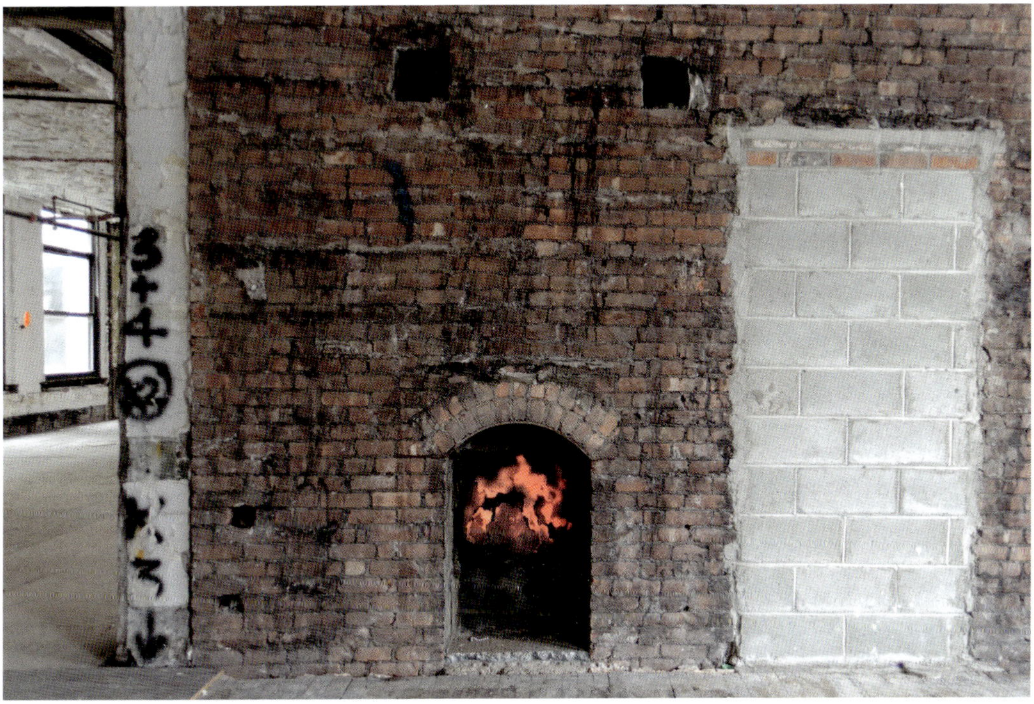

Many of the rooms in 5 Beekman contain small fireplaces. This one has a fire painted in. It is unclear if these fireplaces remained after the renovations.

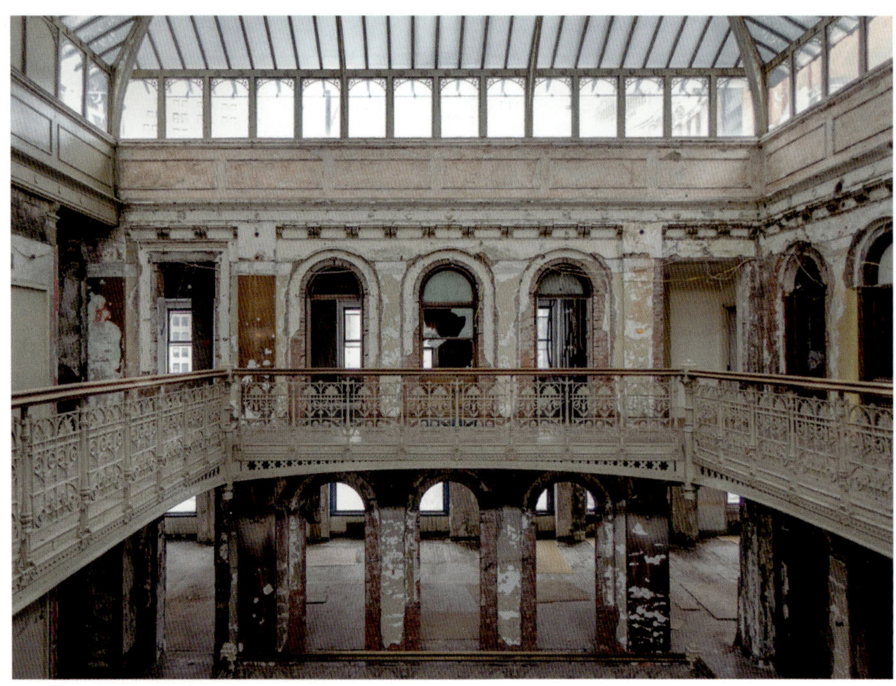

View looking across the balconies of 5 Beekman.

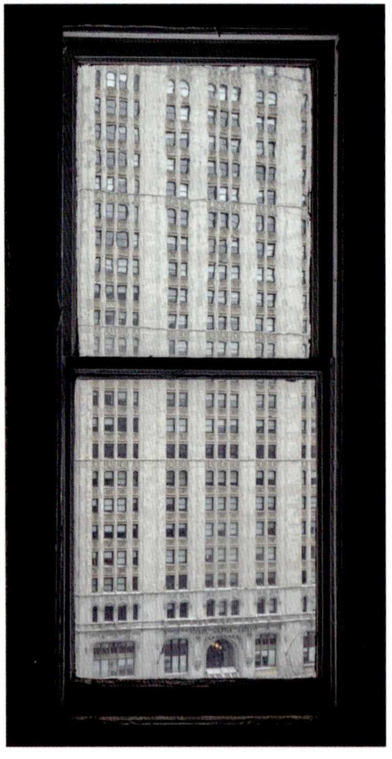

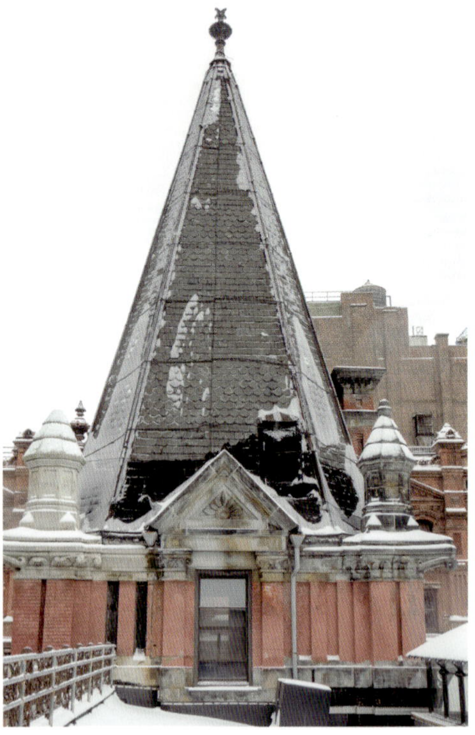

Left: The Woolworth Building is seen through the original wavy glass.

Right: One of two turrets on the roof that has been restored into a high-end hotel room.

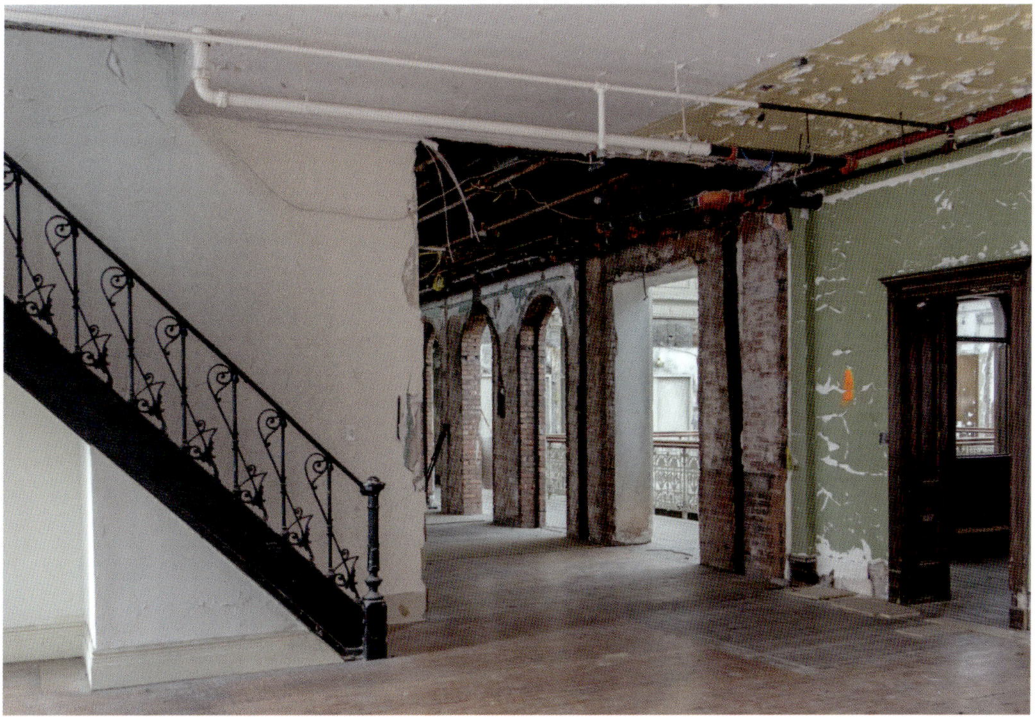

There are numerous rooms that stem off the balconies. Each has arches that are either windows or doorways. This is the top floor; there is a private staircase leading into the turret.

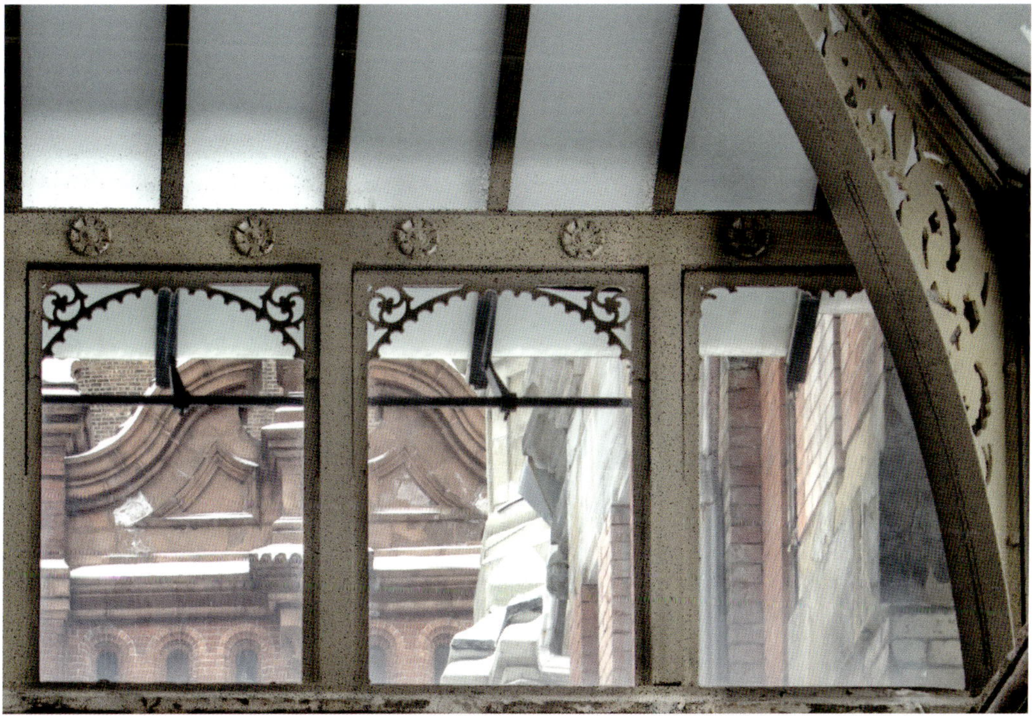

Distinctive cast-iron work holding up the skylight.

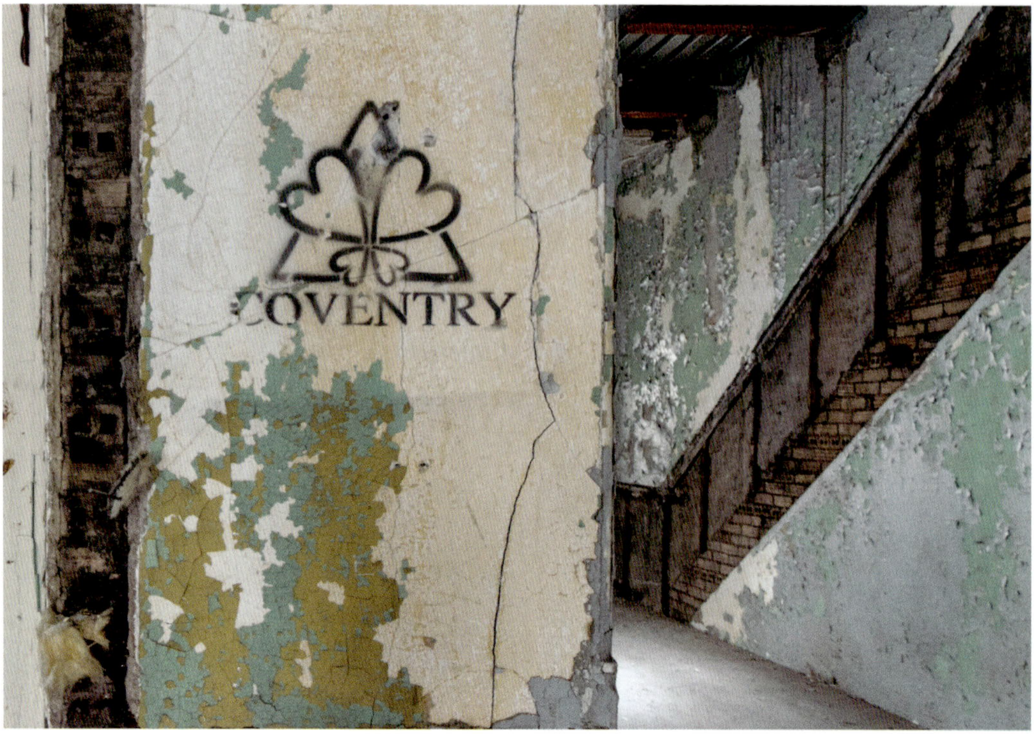

A sign for Coventry, one of the many business that have been tenants here over the years at 5 Beekman.

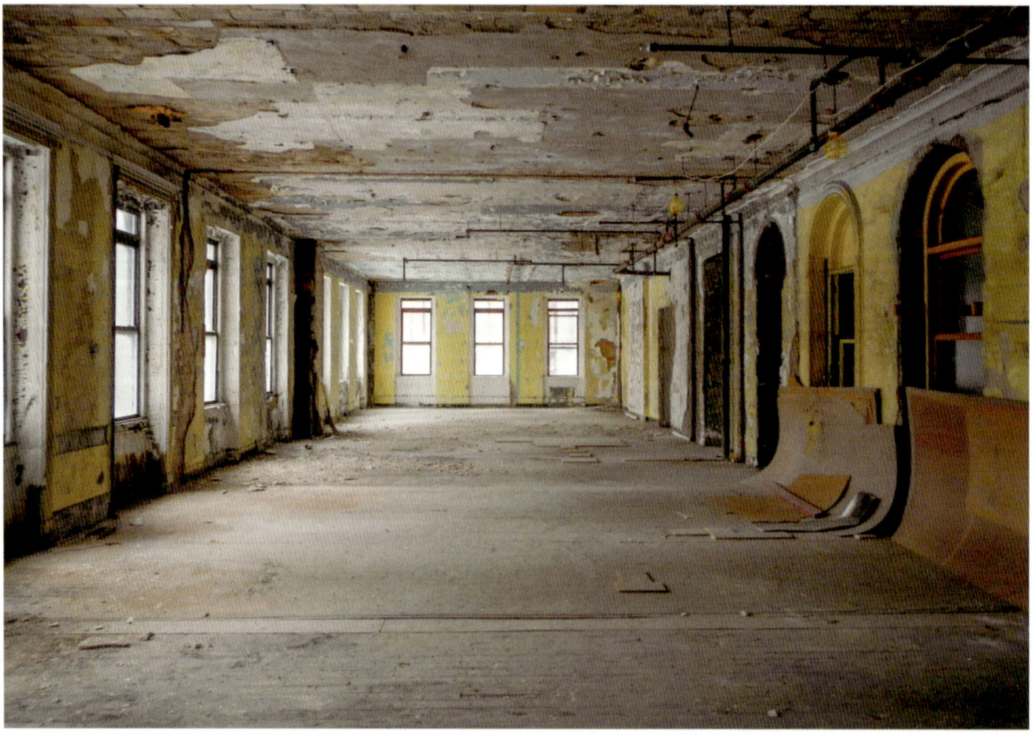

A large room off the atrium will undoubtedly be turned into numerous hotel rooms.

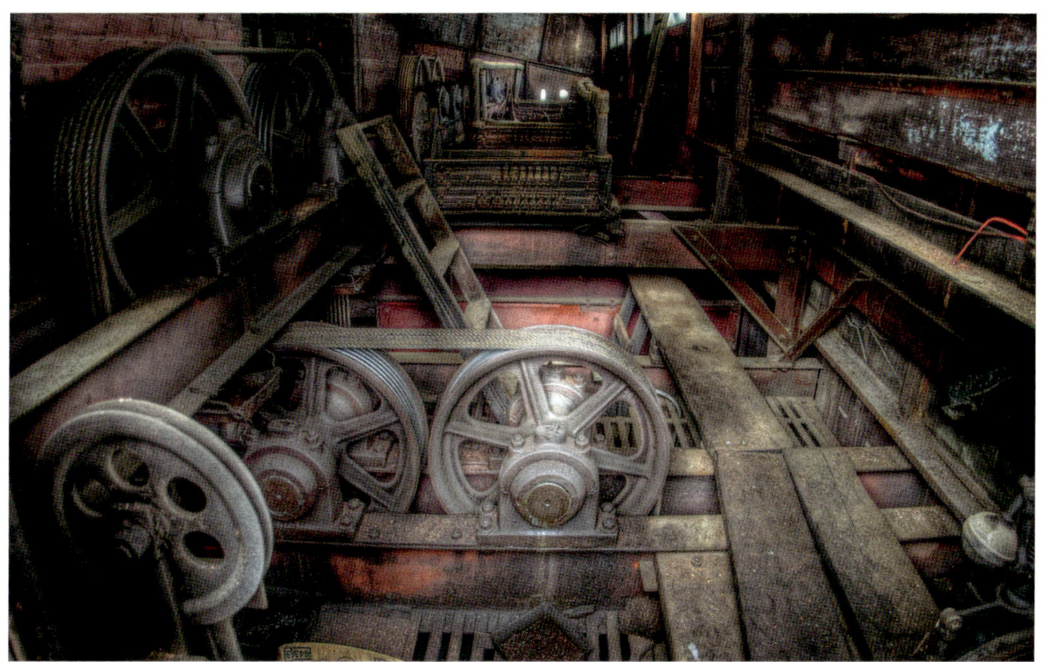

Above: The elevator mechanism at 5 Beekman can be accessed via a panel from the roof. Five Beekman was the third building in New York to have an elevator.

Right: The exterior of 5 Beekman today. The building has been beautifully restored to its former opulence and includes the Temple Court Bar Room in the atrium, 287 hotel guest rooms, and a gym.

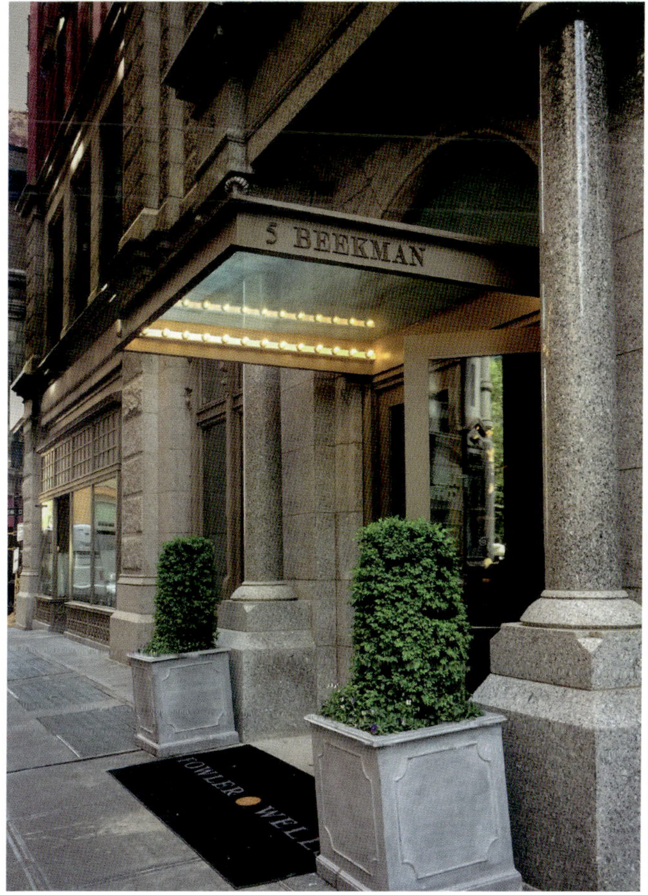

2

WOOLWORTH BUILDING

The elegant edifice of the Woolworth Building graces lower Manhattan and was once the tallest building in the world (upon completion in 1913 until the construction of the Chrysler Building and the Empire State Building in 1930 and 1931). Millionaire Frank W. Woolworth financed the building in cash, amassing his fortune through his iconic Woolworth stores. Architect Gilbert Cass designed the building in the Beaux Arts style and won acclaim for the forward-thinking steel frame and the building's stunning appearance. Although never technically abandoned, the building was off-limits to the general public for many years and had many abandoned areas inside.

The Woolworth Building won accolades for its opulent interior, including a high-ceilinged lobby with mosaics, sculptures, and a gold-decked ceiling. The lobby features gargoyle type statues (*aka* grotesques) of Woolworth himself counting his dimes and architect Gilbert Cass hugging the building, among others involved in the construction. It was one of the first buildings to have an elevator with both local and express options. A structure such as this with sixty floors would not be possible without a bank of elevators with this sort of feature.

Initially, the exterior was clad in terra cotta tiles, which were removed due to rot and excessive maintenance costs. Gargoyles and grotesques adorn the exterior. (Gargoyles have a very specific purpose as downspouts; any other decorative resembling a gargoyle is called a grotesque.) Thirty-two gargoyles were casualties of the tile removal. The top floors were exquisitely capped in copper, which turned the characteristic green patina.

Fireproofing in the new era of skyscrapers became an issue in the construction industry. The Equitable Life building burned in 1912, despite the claim that it was fireproof. This fire, that killed six, drew attention to buildings needing fireproofing and other safety precautions. Unlike the original Beekman building, the Woolworth building was fireproofed from the start of construction.

In 1998, the Woolworth building was sold to the Witkoff Group. The top thirty floors were again sold off in 2012. This developer turned the top twenty-five floors of the building tower into thirty-four luxury apartments with hefty price tags in the $7 to $10 million range. Two listed at $20 million. The seven-level, 9,700-square-foot Woolworth Pinnacle Penthouse ("Castle in the Sky") had a New York City residential record-busting $110 million price in 2017. As of November 2019, it was still for sale at a reduced price of $79 million. The tower residences have an indoor pool (which was previously abandoned) and a separate lobby entrance for the mere masses' access.

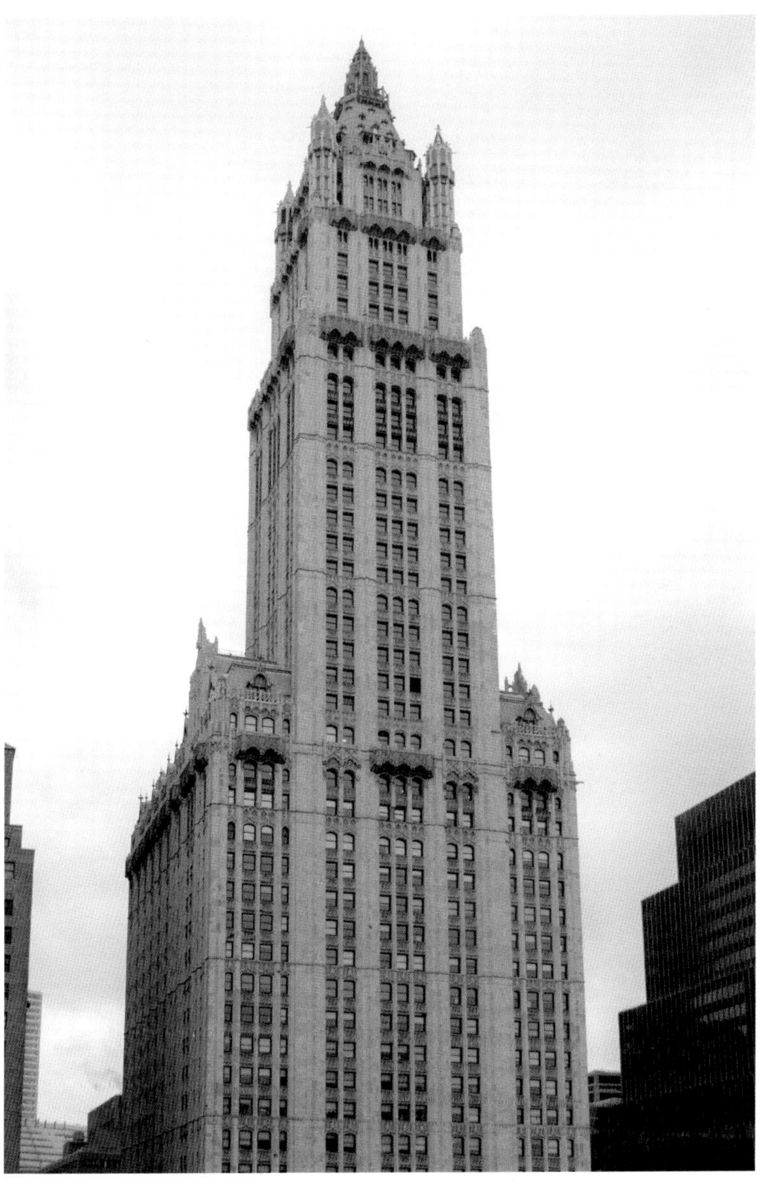

The exterior of the F. W. Woolworth building in Lower Manhattan.

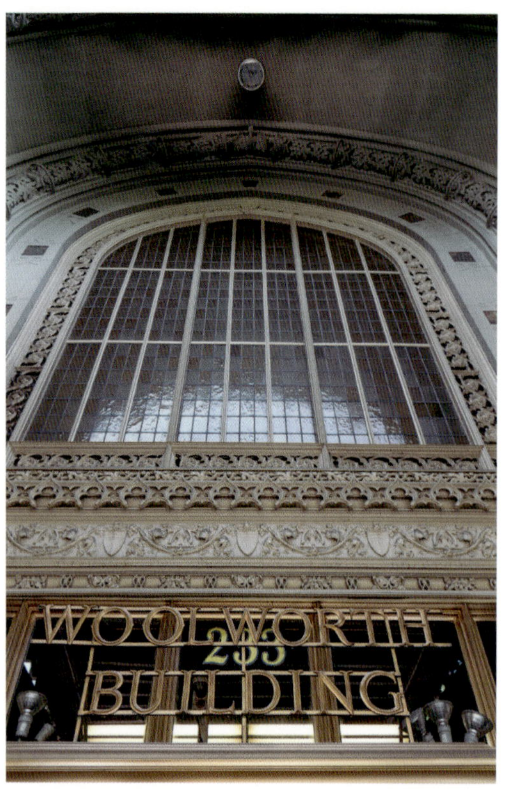

Front facade of the Woolworth Building.

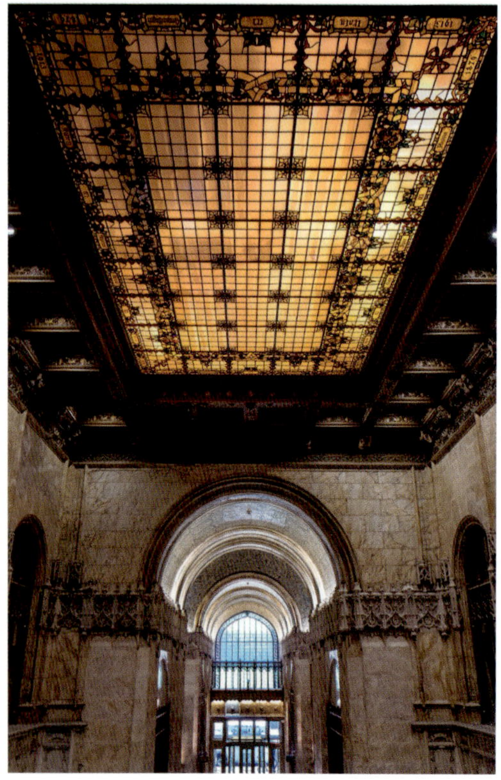

The front door of the Woolworth Building and a massive overhead Beaux Arts stained-glass skylight above.

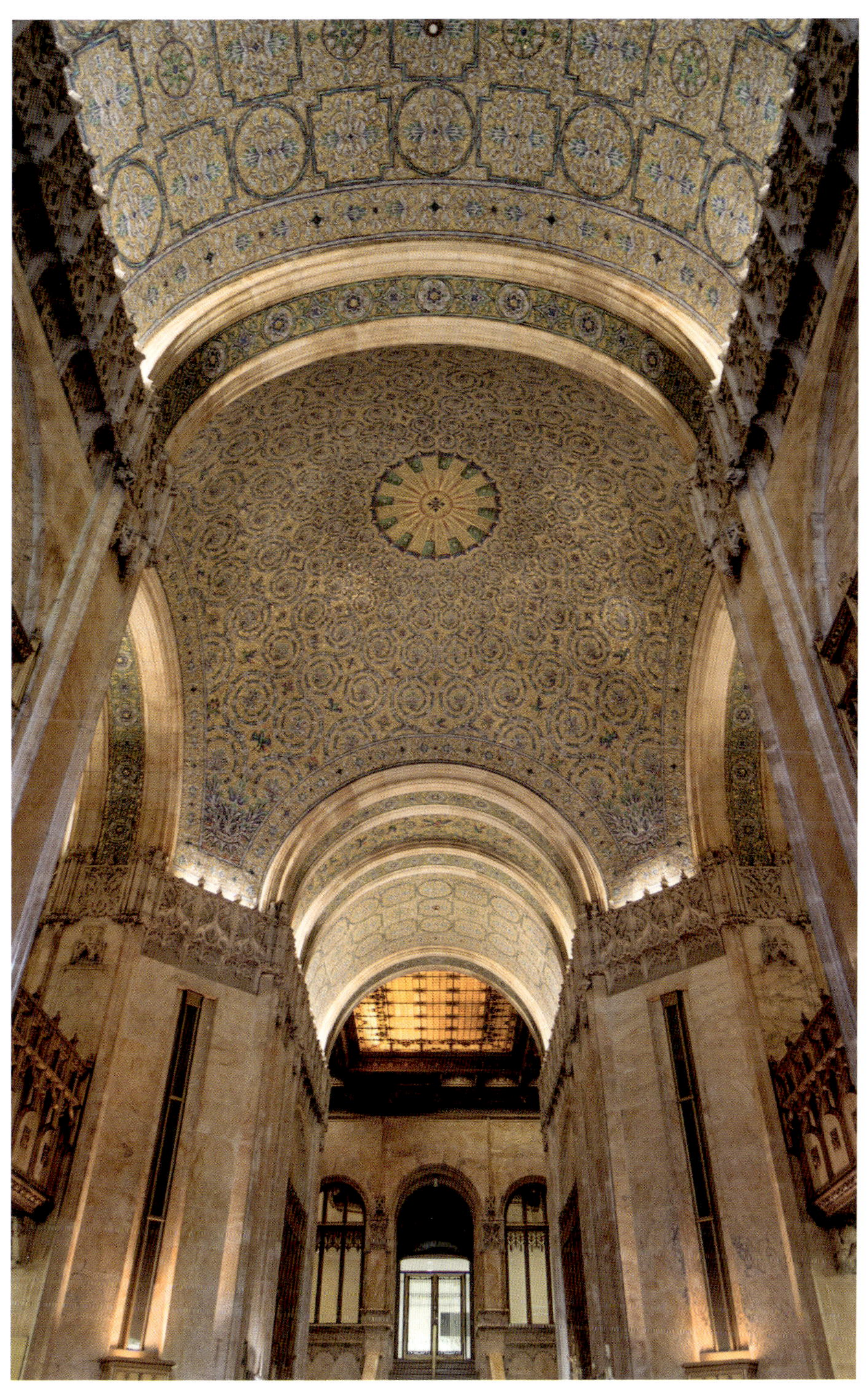

The interior of the Woolworth Building has a vaulted ceiling of gold gilt.

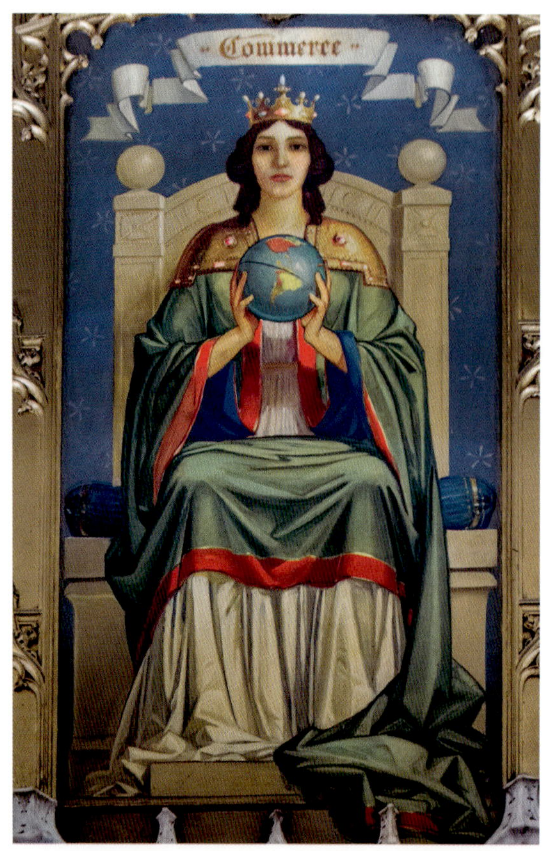

A painting of Commerce adorns the inside the lobby of the Woolworth Building. The building was known as the "Cathedral of Commerce," meant to inspire upward movement by its height and opulence.

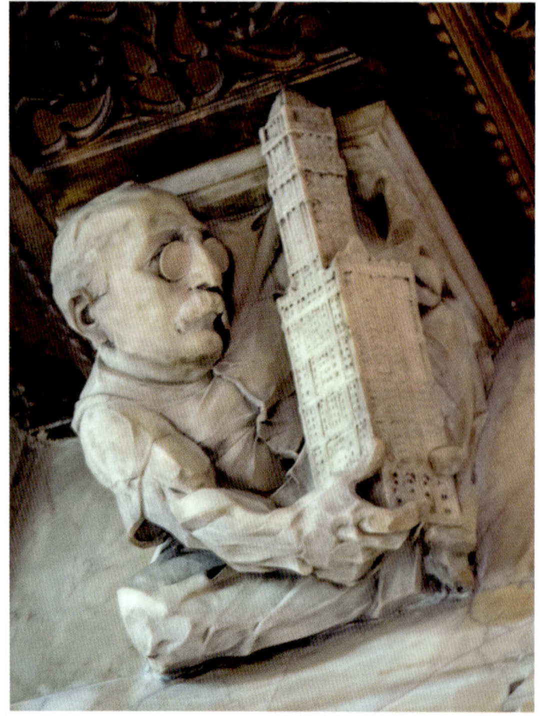

An interior grotesque depicts Cass Gilbert, the architect of the Woolworth Building. There are several of these figures inside the Woolworth Building, many of the people central to the construction of the building. Additional statues include Engineer Gunvald Aus taking a girder's measurements and Louis Horowitz, the builder, on that newfangled machine called the telephone.

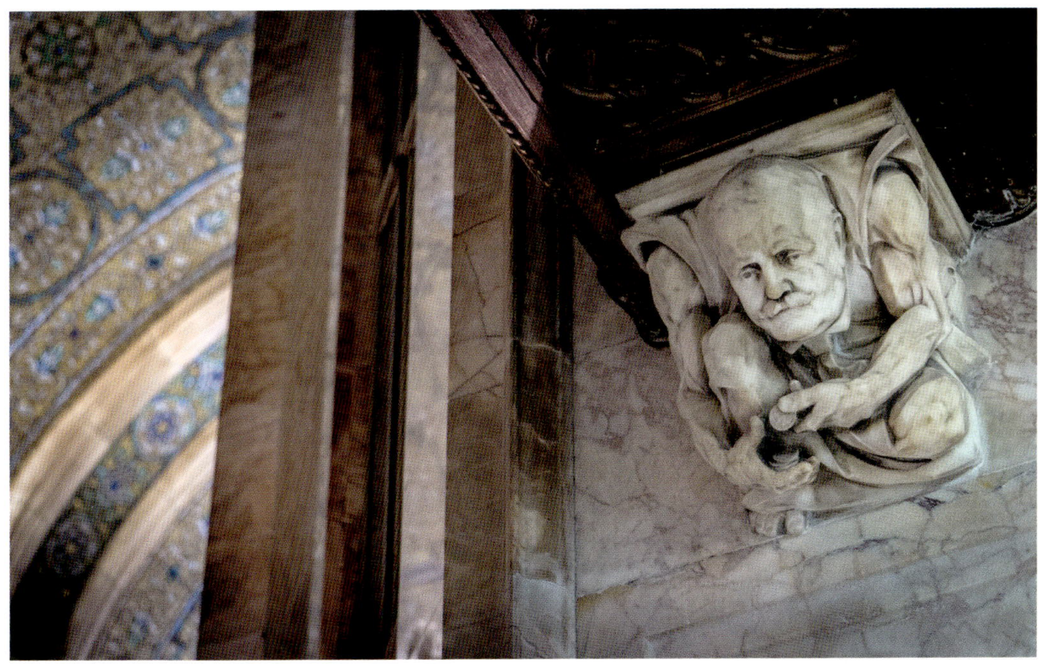

A grotesque on the interior of the Woolworth Building depicts Frank W. Woolworth counting his coins to pay for his grand building in New York City.

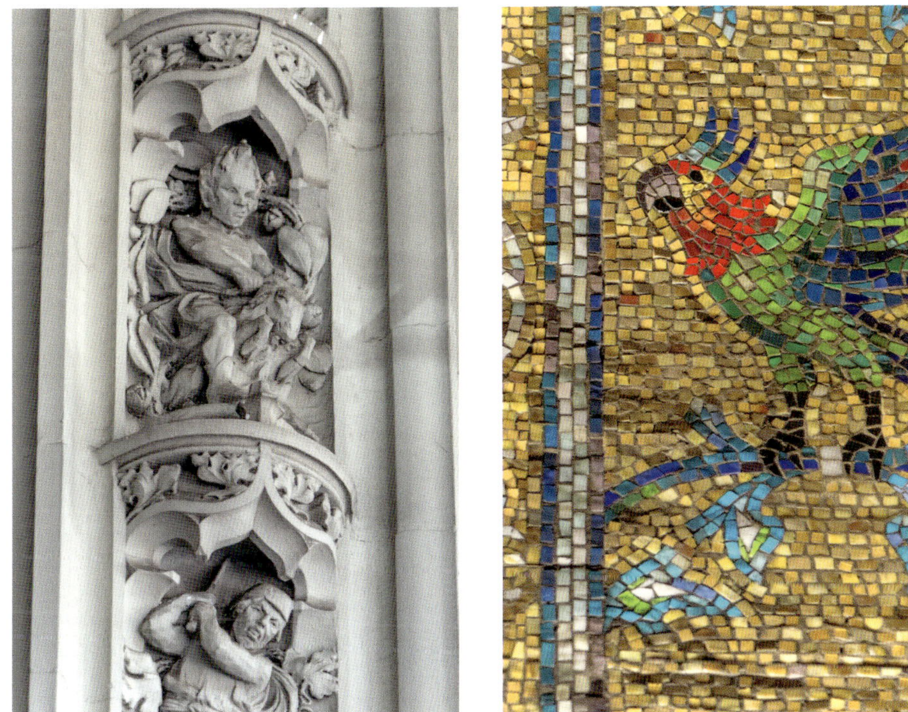

Left: Other grotesques also adorn columns on the interior of the building.

Right: Detail of a mosaic, part of the Woolworth Building's enormous vaulted ceiling in the lobby.

3

BROOKLYN NAVY YARD

It took far too long for anyone to notice that the Brooklyn Navy Yard was a prime piece of real estate wasting away. I got there just in time, before every abandoned building had been renovated. Alas, I was a little too late for some buildings, but I believe I got the gist of the place.

Established in 1801, the Brooklyn Navy Yard served as the United States' premier naval shipbuilding facility for 165 years. The yard was in continuous operation until 1966. Defense Secretary McNamara under President Lyndon Johnson decommissioned it, even though the yard still employed 9,000 workers. The Navy then sold it to the City of New York. The shipyard once produced famous battleships, including the USS *Maine*, the USS *Missouri*, the USS *Niagara*, and the USS *Arizona*. The industrial yard is once again a bustling work center and houses over 330 businesses. A brand new Wegman's grocery store opened recently, and one can now take the new water taxi to the yard and see the dry docks that still operate today.

The yard was America's most important shipbuilding site; even during the Civil War, it employed 6,000 men. Vital to the war effort during World War II, peak activity occurred when 70,000 people worked at the yard. Many men were overseas fighting, so women were trained to be mechanics and technicians. The yard was the first Navy facility to employ women in such positions. In 1960, a fire during the construction of the aircraft carrier USS *Constellation* killed fifty and injured 323, tarnishing the yard's reputation.

The Brooklyn Navy Yard also contains a hospital, called the Naval Hospital or Naval Annex. Decommissioned in the 1970s, this hospital, which was also active during the Civil War, employed some of the first female nurses and medical students in the United States Navy. Steiner Film Studios now leases the hospital property, with the hospital currently inaccessible for the time being. There is also a cemetery located on the hospital grounds, and although the site closed in 1910 and human remains interred at other cemeteries, some human remains were discovered as recently as 1997. The landscape recently opened as a green space in the yard.

The revitalization of the yard includes some very eco-friendly businesses. The yard contains a rooftop winery and a rooftop farm, which also includes an apiary with bee-keeping classes. IceStone, a Navy Yard tenant since 2000, manufacturers recycled glass countertops. Solar panels and wind turbines power the streetlights. The Navy Yard is also home to numerous startups, small businesses, tech companies, and artisans. It is poised to be one of the largest urban manufacturing centers in the country. You can visit the Navy Yard via the new ferry for the low price of a single subway fare. It is an excellent deal.

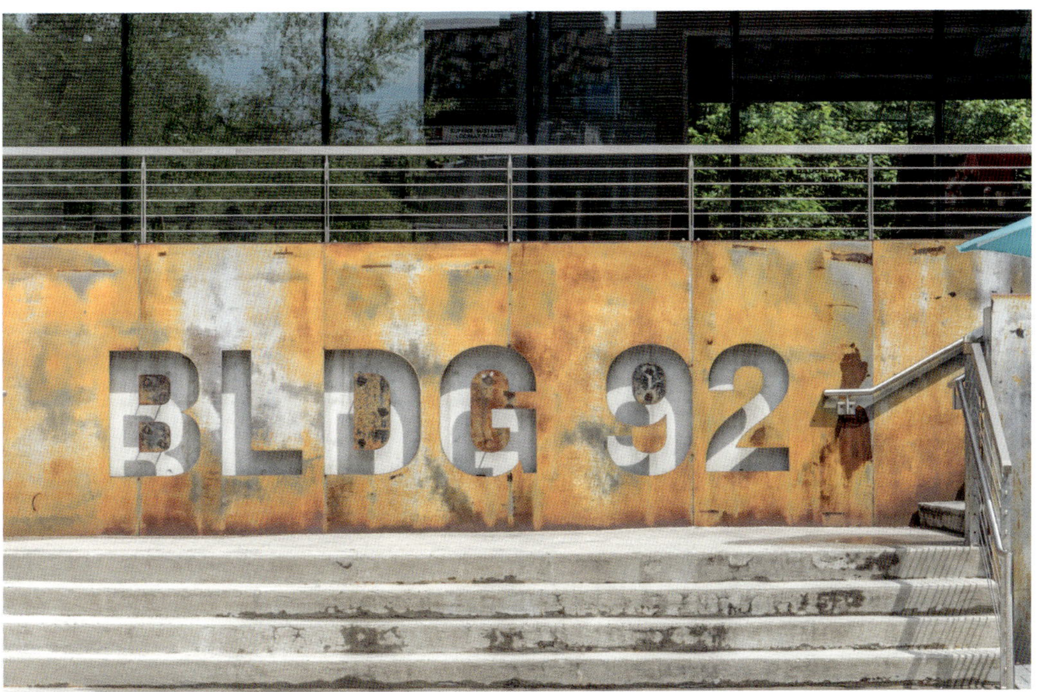

Building 92 at the Brooklyn Navy Yard is the last standing building of a Marine Barracks. This building was designed to be used as U.S. Marine Corps Commandant's Residence in 1858.

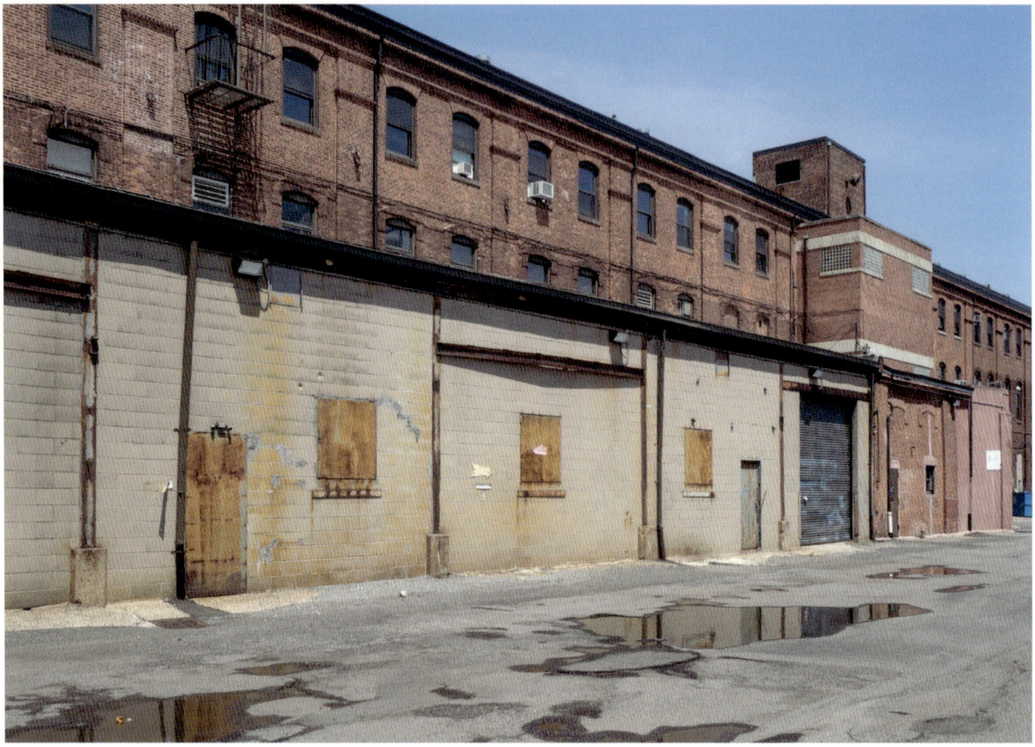

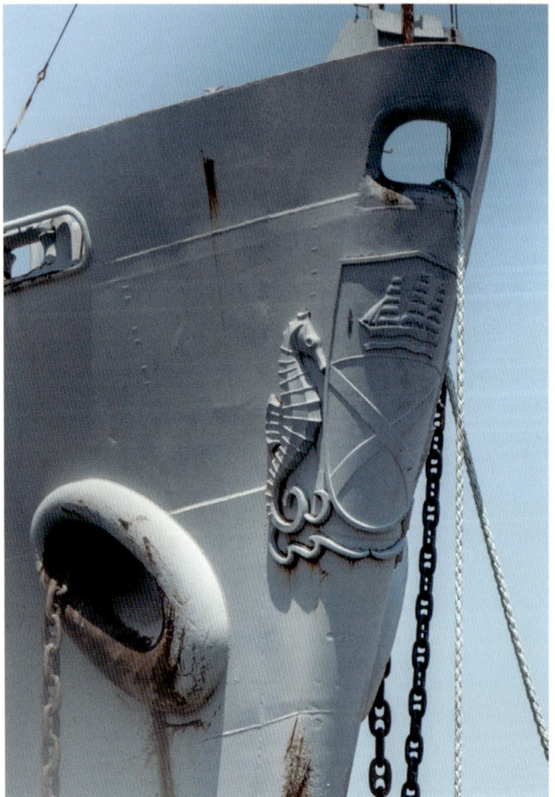

Above: Most of the buildings at the Navy Yard have been repurposed rather than newly constructed.

Left: A decorative flourish on the front of a ship at the Brooklyn Navy Yard.

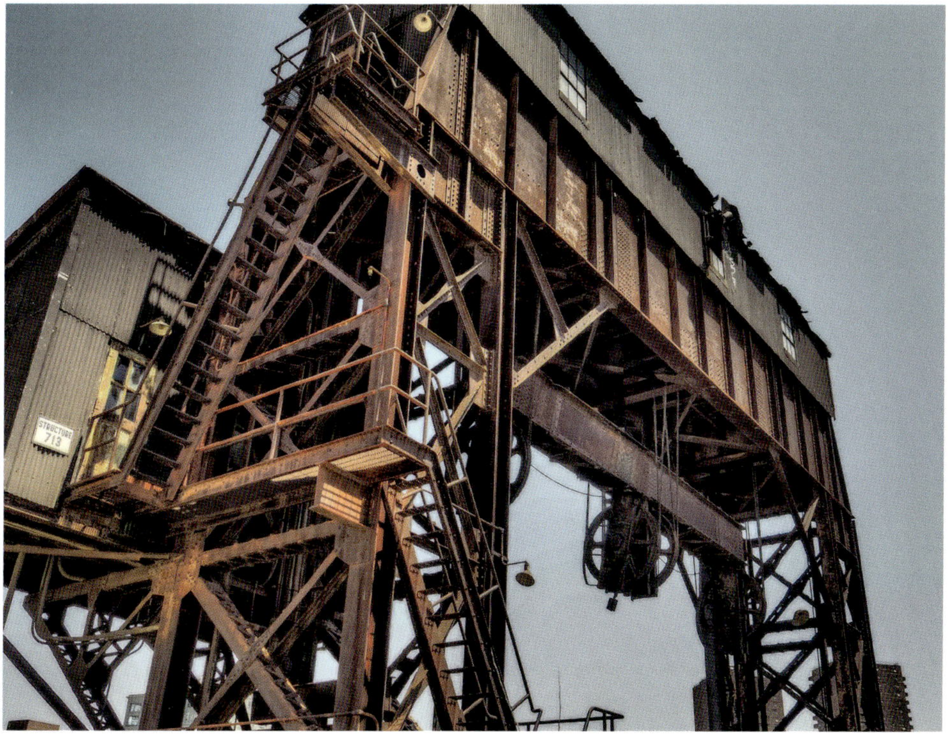

A smaller dry dock for shipbuilding contains this crane.

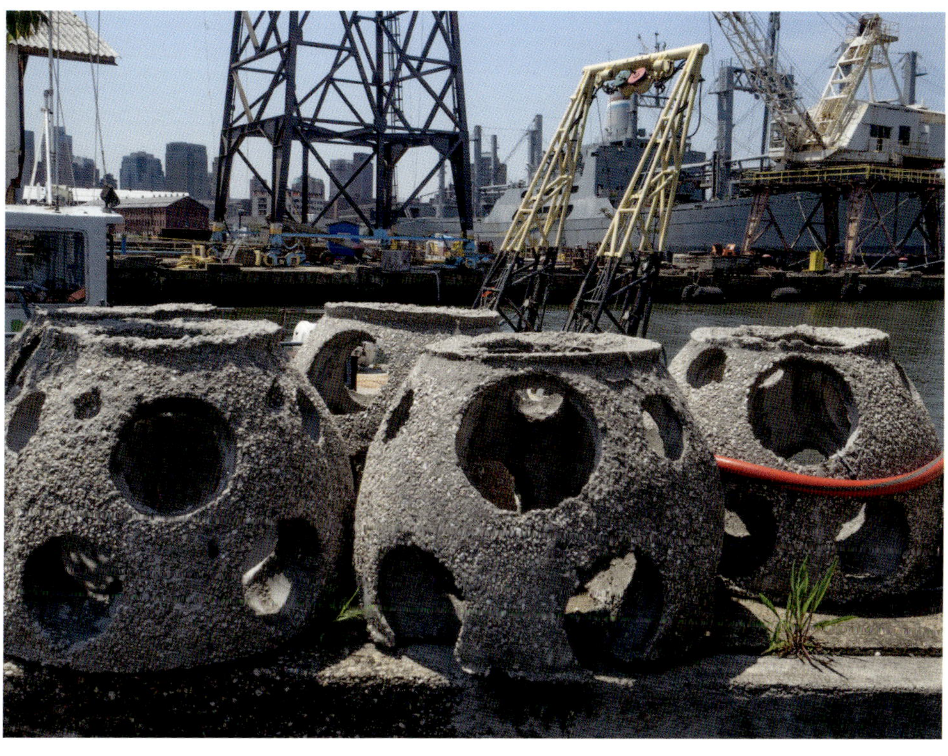

Concrete anchors keep piers in place.

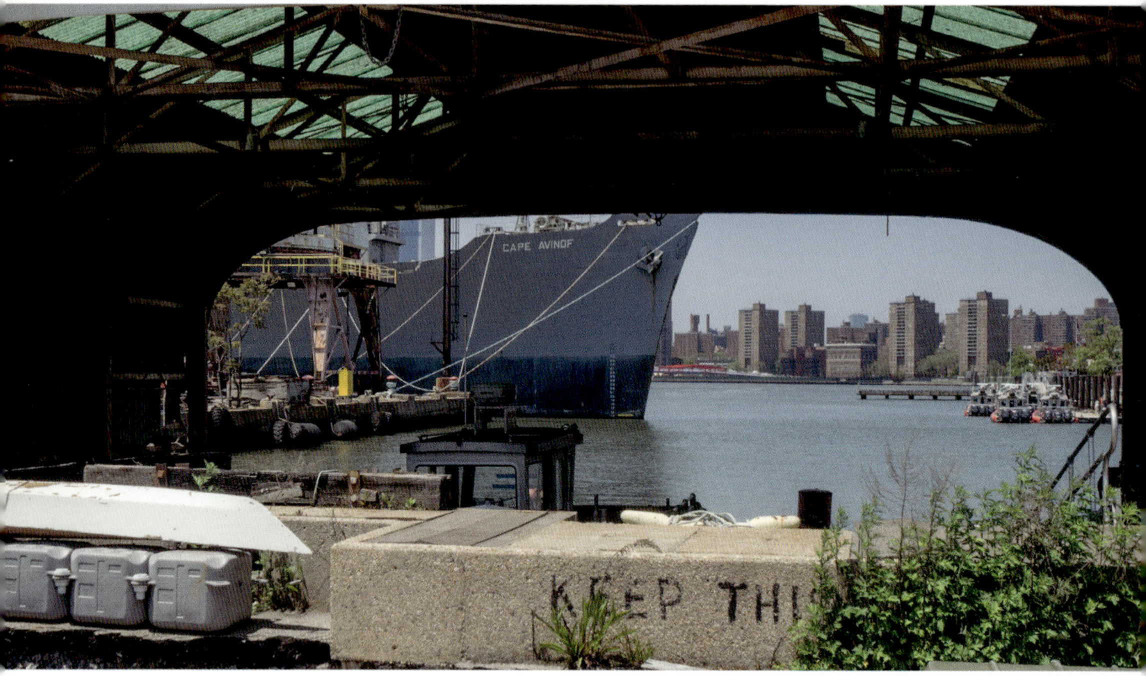

A view through a building shows part of a dry dock, ships, and Brooklyn in the distance.

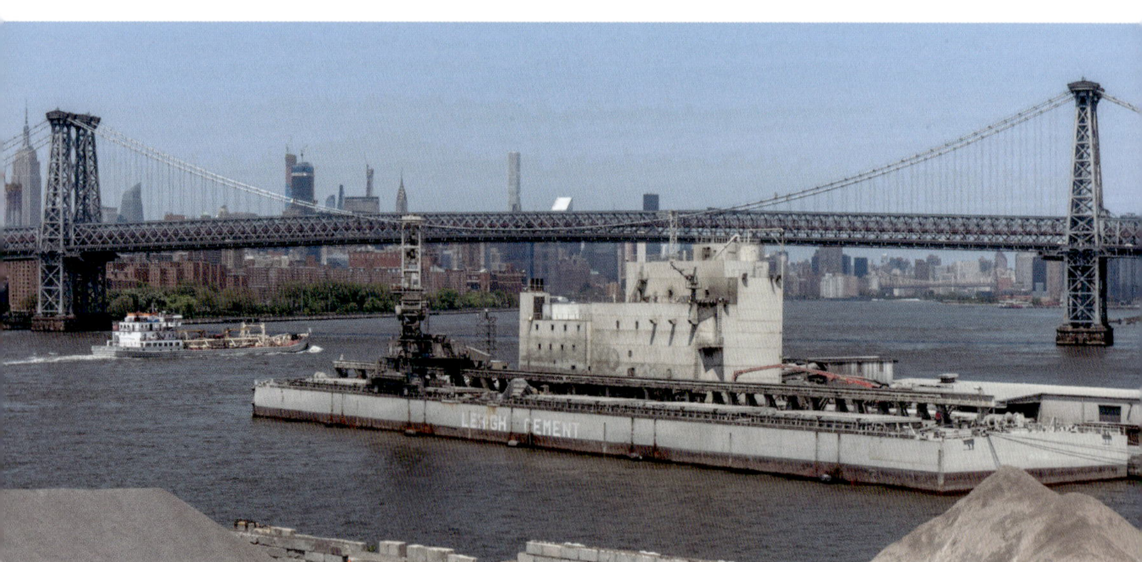

View from the Brooklyn Navy Yard looking towards the Williamsburg Bridge.

4

BROOKLYN ARMY TERMINAL

Brooklyn is also home to another old military site, and while the two have a similar history and purpose, they are worlds apart visually. Much like Brooklyn Navy Yard, the Army Terminal, also known as the New York Port of Embarkation, has a history rooted in Brooklyn and World War I and II, and is now also a model urban manufacturing facility. Today, over 100 businesses, mostly small businesses, call the Army Terminal home. Like the Woolworth Building in Lower Manhattan, architect Cass Gilbert designed the Army Terminal. When finished, the terminal was the largest concrete building in the world and was longer than the Woolworth Building was tall. The highlight of the terminal is the atrium in Building B, the larger of two buildings.

The government completed the Army Terminal in 1919, after WWI. The terminal was mainly used for deploying troops and supplies. Supplies arriving by train would be offloaded by crane inside the building, loaded onto one of the many balconies in the atrium according to its destination country, which was painted on the wall, then processed through state-of-the-art cargo processing. During World War II, the Terminal employed 20,000 workers, with 3.2 million troops deployed from this location. Troops arrived by train, and would ascend ramps putting them onto the appropriate outbound ship. Elvis Presley, the most famous of the troops departing from the Navy Terminal, held a press conference in front of a crowd of fans and reporters before leaving for an eighteen-month tour of Germany in 1958.

The Brooklyn Army Terminal was purchased by the City of New York in 1981. After being decommissioned in the 1970s, the terminal sat empty until the 1980s. Much like the Brooklyn Navy Yard, the transformation is nearly complete and nearly full with tenants. The terminal features a recently renovated Food Manufacturing Hub for small food manufacturing firms and a Micro Manufacturing Hub. Many garment and clothing businesses are also located here.

The terminal is composed of two large buildings and an administration building, and constructed with concrete slabs and rebar. The blocky cement interiors reminded me of the Brutalist style of architecture. The larger building features a massive atrium capped by a glass skylight. A large overhead mobile crane operated in the atrium to move cargo. I believe that Architect Cass Gilbert, better known for ornate Beaux Arts styles of architecture, definitely designed this building with the architectural rule "form follows function."

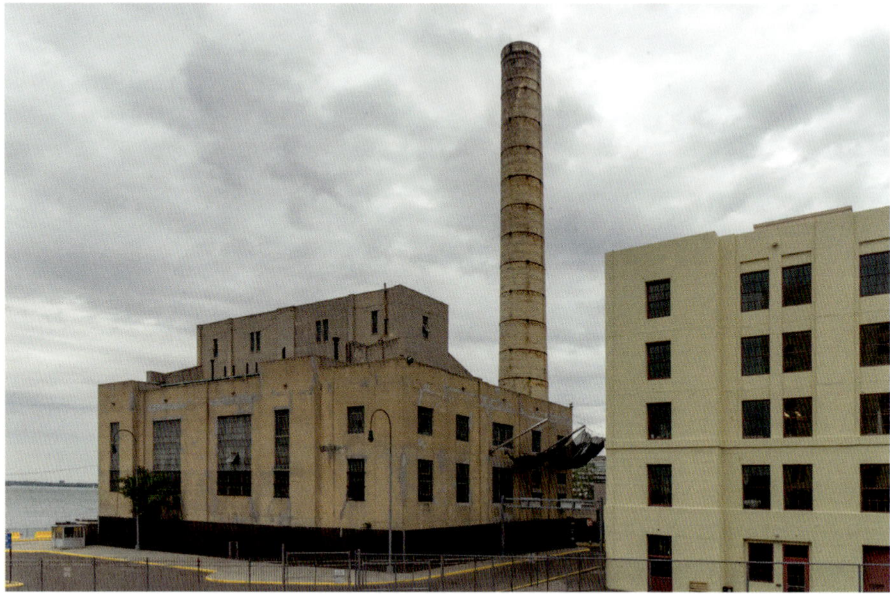

Exterior of two buildings at Brooklyn Army Terminal.

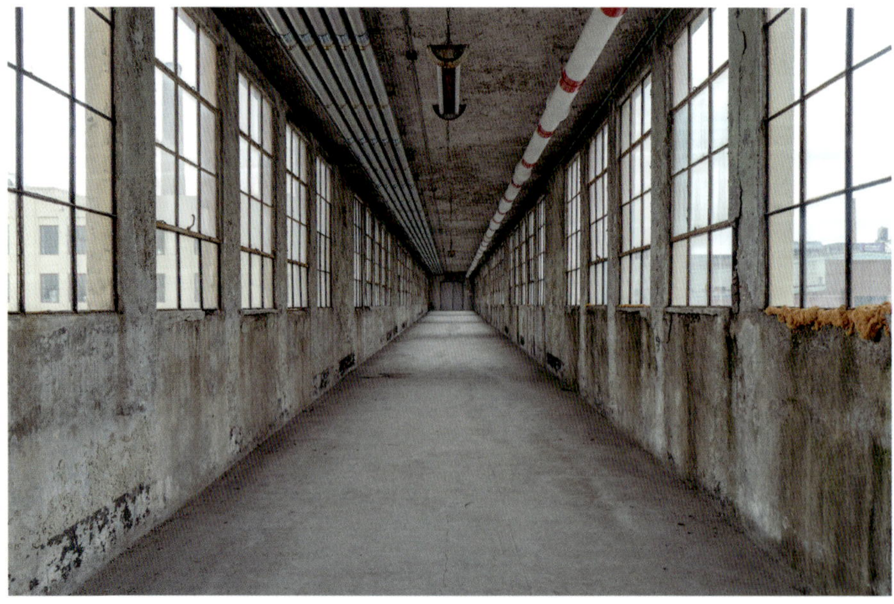

A skyway connects the two main buildings of the Brooklyn Army Terminal.

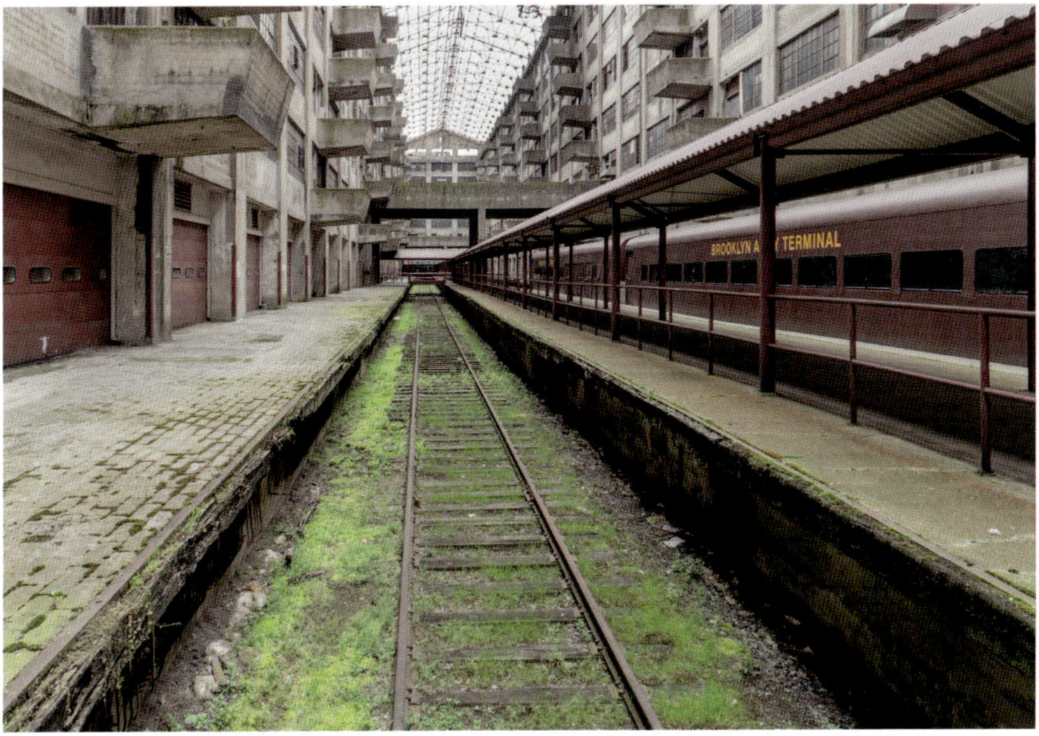

Above: This train inside the Atrium of Building B is for show; it is not an original train. This platform is where troops left for overseas posts during WWII.

Right: These balconies in the atrium on the Navy Terminal were used to collect imported goods with the assistance of a giant overhead crane.

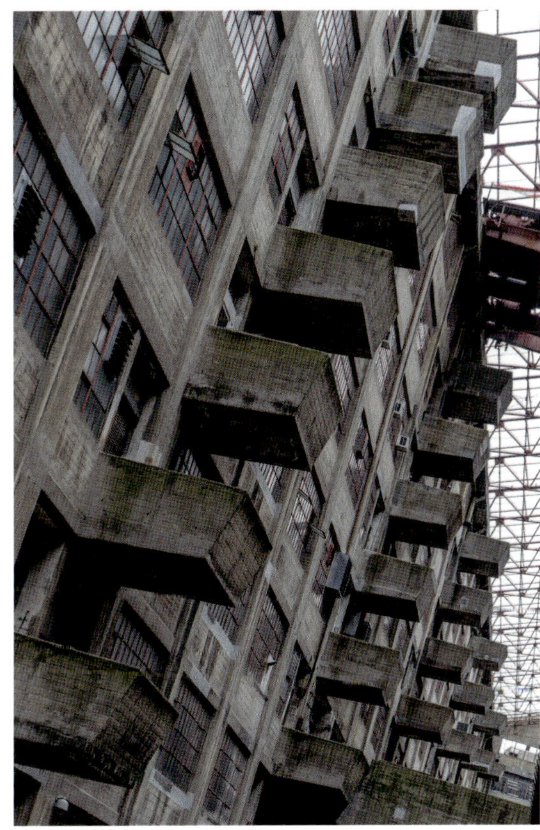

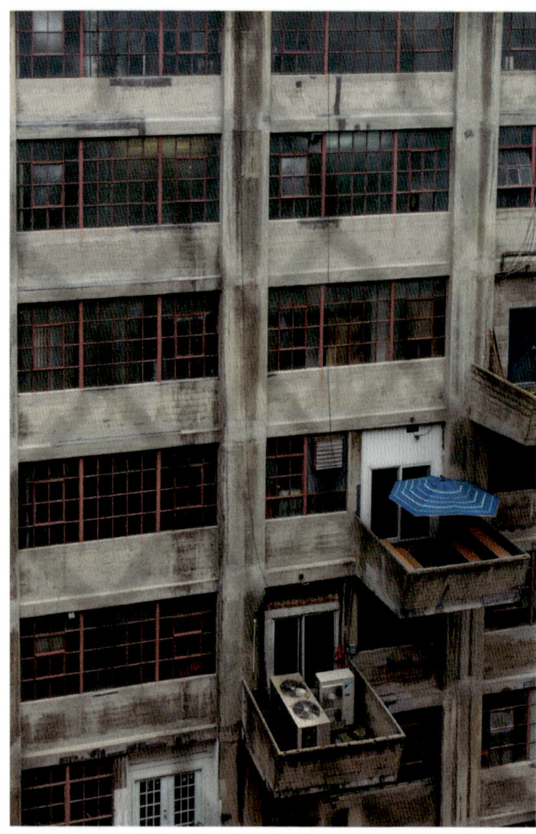

Balconies now are used by the individual tenants, who are mostly small manufacturers.

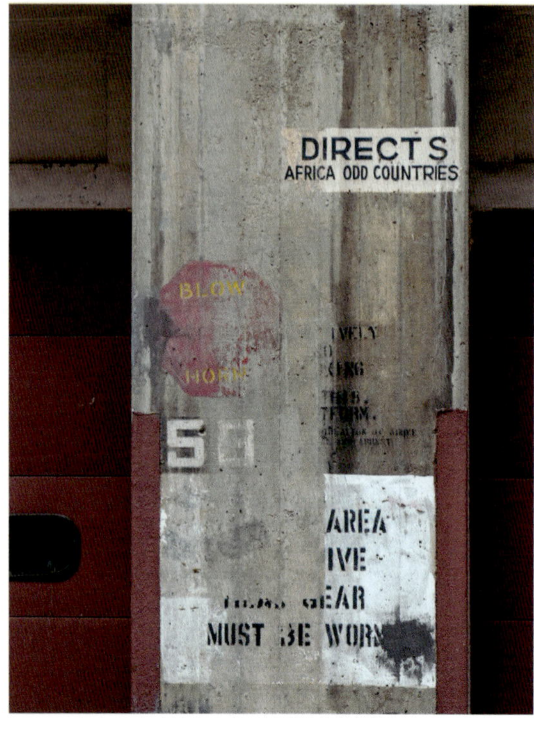

Posts along the tracks are painted with destination countries that received the goods being shipped.

5

DOMINO SUGAR REFINERY

A large smokestack looms ominously along the Brooklyn waterfront next to the Williamsburg Bridge. It belongs to the Domino Sugar Refinery, and what is known now as Domino Park. Constructed in 1856, the refinery was once the most productive sugar refinery in the world. Daily, the factory refined four million pounds of raw sugar from Cuba and the Caribbean, much it cut by slaves. Collectively, the Domino factories refined almost 98% of all sugar in the United States, and the Brooklyn factory was the largest producer during that time. The New York site was crucial to the growth of the surrounding neighborhood of Williamsburg, and also to Brooklyn in general as a manufacturing center of New York and the country. The refinery employed as many as 4,500 workers, many of them immigrants who arrived on the shores of Ellis Island earlier.

I imagine not many people think about where the sugar in their morning coffee comes from, but sugar refining was (and still is) a messy affair. The raw sugar was unloaded and heated to extreme temperatures to dissolve it, putting workers at enormous risk daily. The sugar was then filtered, sometimes using animal bones, crystalized, and finally dried. The packaging was also carried out at the plant, sorted into cubes and packets and other forms. Workers spent long days in different buildings, in various occupations to provide sugar for Americans.

The refinery finally shut its doors in 2004, sat abandoned, and became a reminder of the neighborhood's industrial past that was now supplanted by and white-collar workers, artists, and musicians. In 2014, before most of the sugar plant was demolished to make way for a multi-use development that included a park, affordable housing, and retail, artist Kara Walker installed a massive sculpture made of sugar cubes. The massive installation, entitled *A Subtlcty, or the Marvelous Sugar Baby [an Homage to the unpaid and overworked Artisans who have refined our Sweet tastes from the cane fields to the Kitchens of the New World on the Occasion of the demolition of the Domino Sugar Refining Plant]*, was 75 feet long. Lines snaked around the block to see the eccentric exhibit. The art depicted an enormous Sphinx-like African-American woman made of white sugar surrounded by a dozen or so small basket-wielding children, about five feet tall. Most of these children were made of sugar or molasses, which is a black gooey byproduct of sugar refining. As time went on, these sugar babies deteriorated in disturbing ways. It was a strong statement about the past reliance on slave labor.

Adjacent to the Domino Sugar building lies Domino Park, a new park that preserves some of the old artifacts of the refinery including screw conveyors, bucket conveyors, hoist bridges, Gantry cranes, raw sugar warehouse columns, and four of the syrup tanks. The 80-foot-tall Gantry cranes were used to unload raw sugarcane from freight ships for storage at the warehouse. The main building has been gutted and transformed into office space. The once-imposing neon sign identified the Domino Sugar refinery underwent preservation, as did the exterior of the building. Some of the park's features include an elevated walkway, a dog run, and fountains.

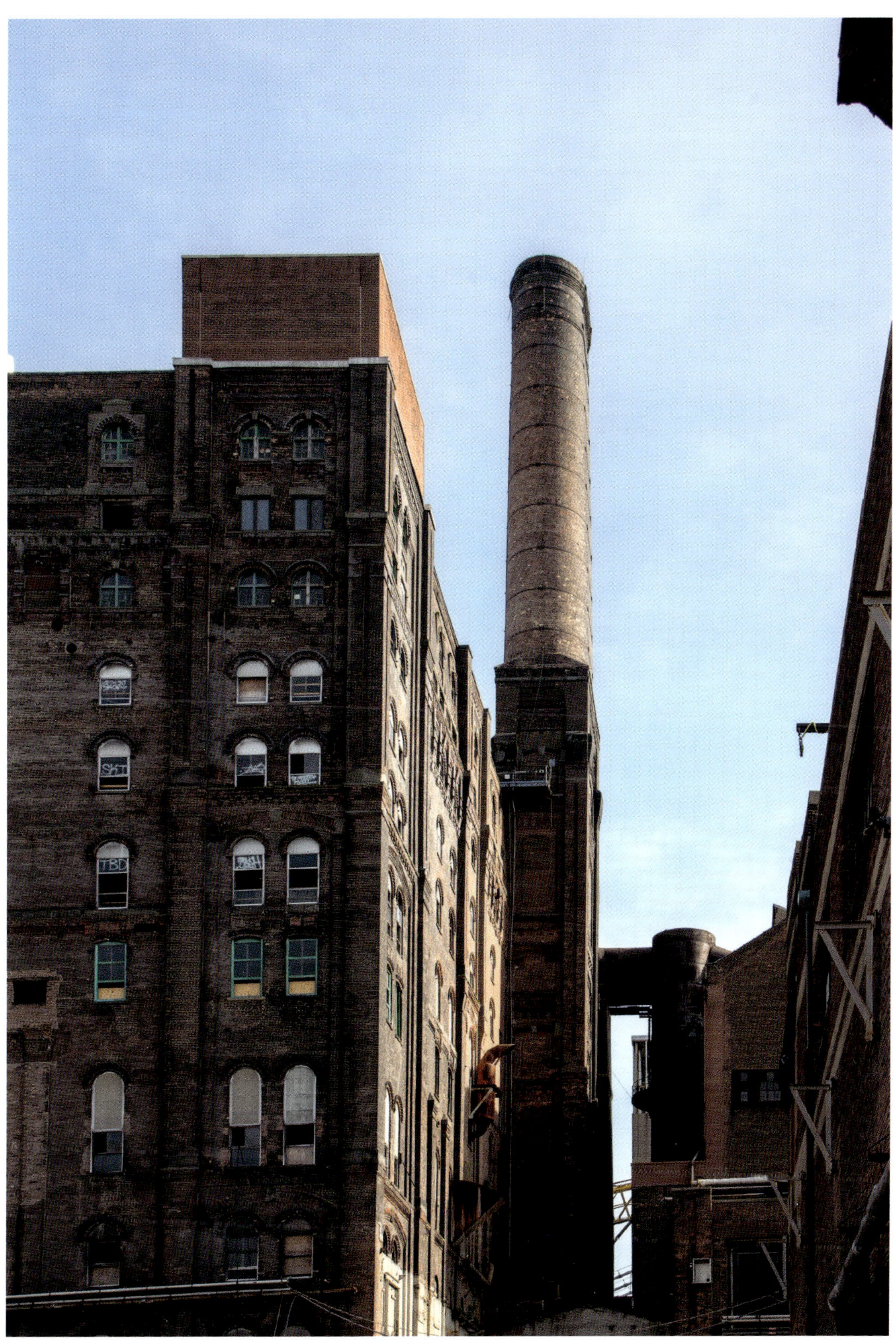

The Domino Sugar refinery took up an entire city block.

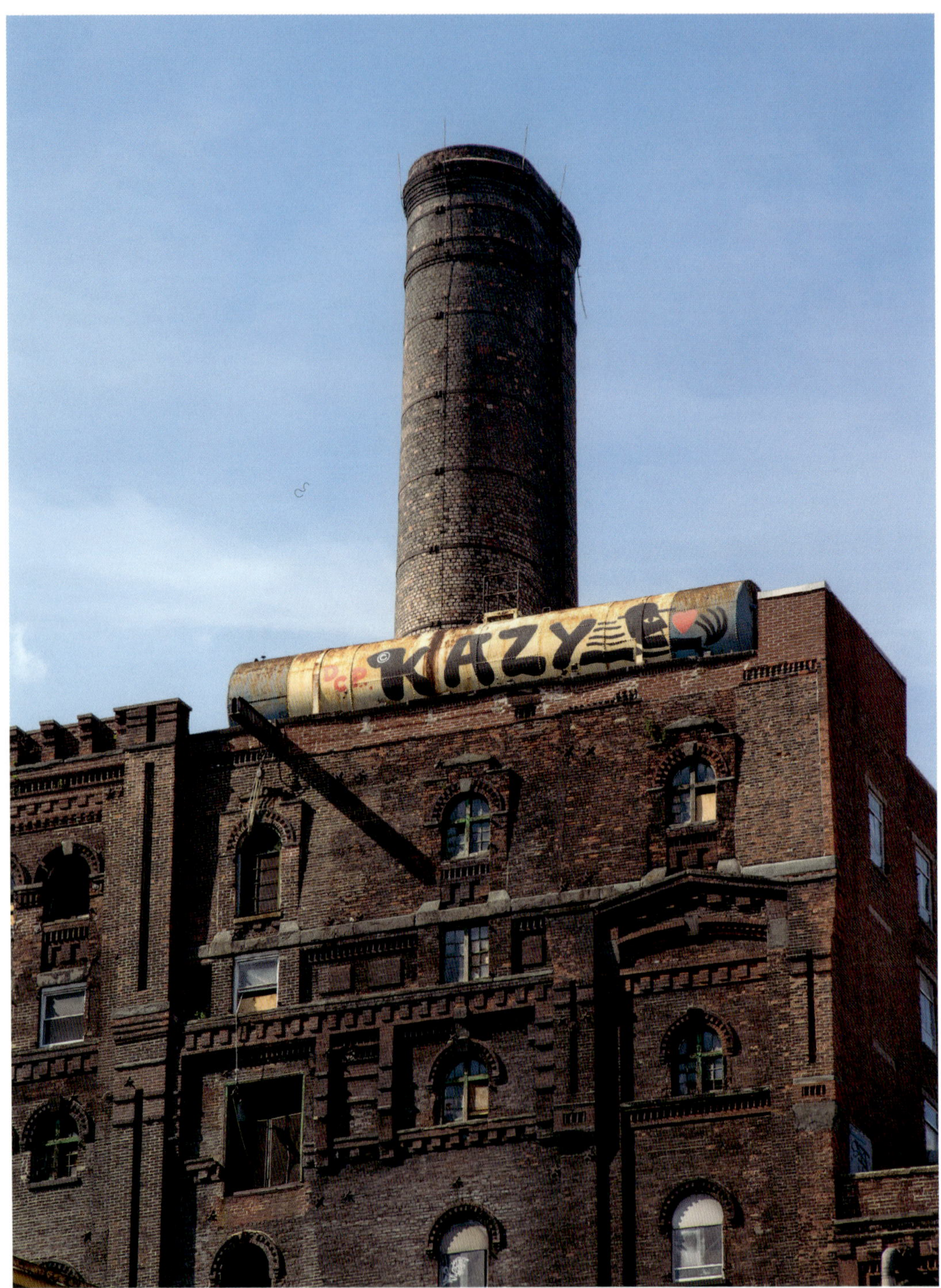

This building has achieved landmark status and as such, is the only original building still standing. The interior was gutted and the exterior walls preserved.

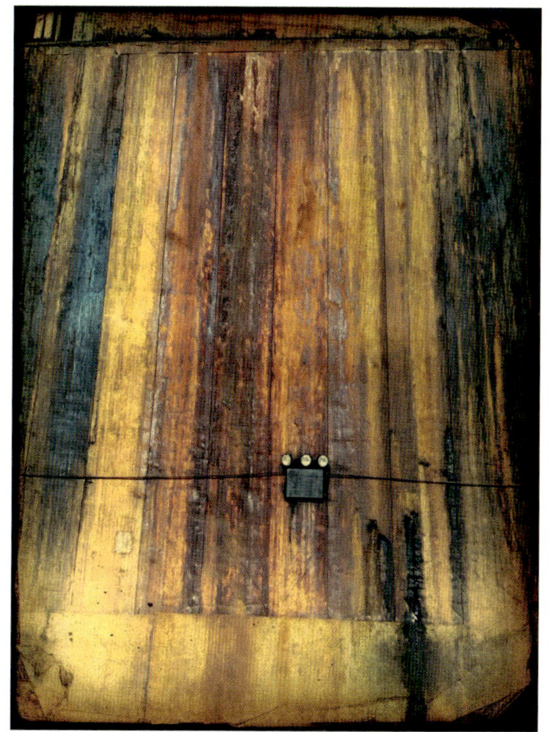

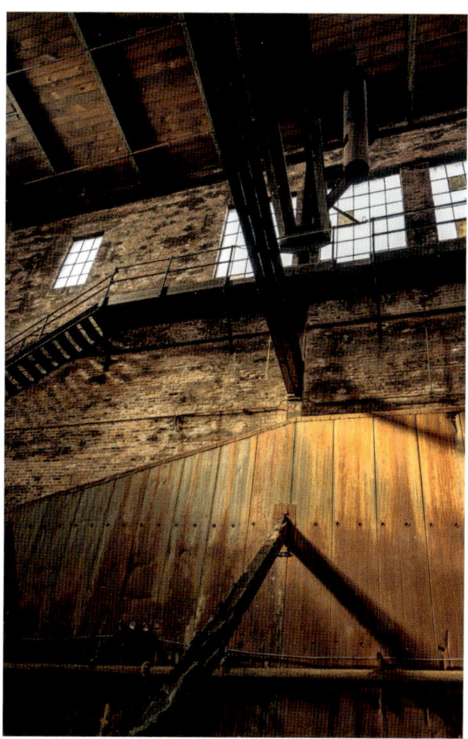

Left: The walls of the inside of this building will be forever stained by years and years of heating raw sugar.

Right: Interior of the sole remaining Domino Sugar building before renovations began.

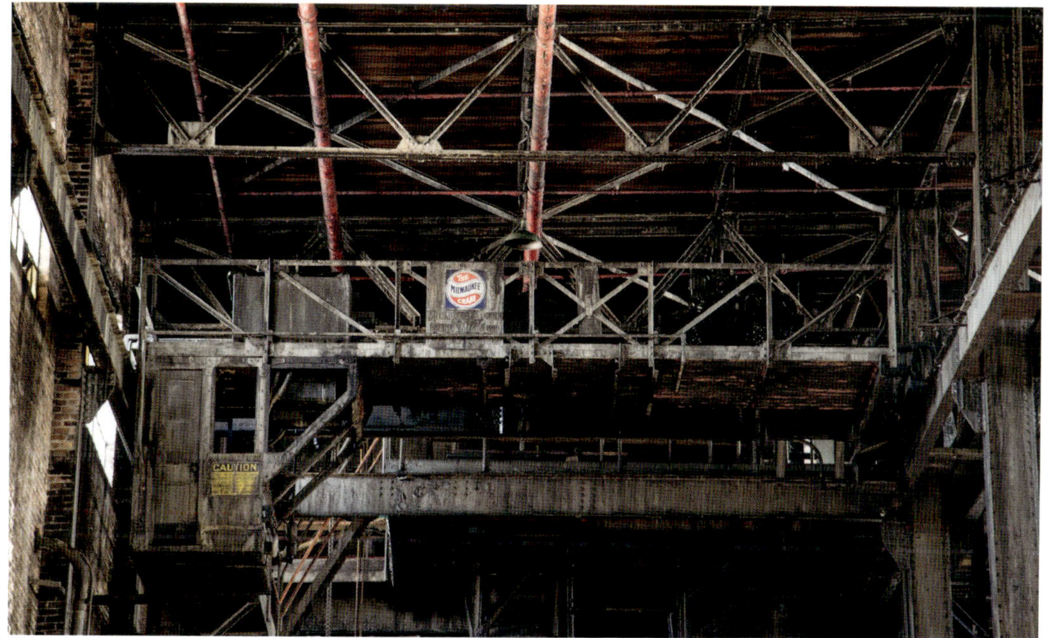

Interior of the Domino Sugar refinery, with all its levels, cranes, and catwalks. The crane was made by the Milwaukee Crane and MFG. Corp.

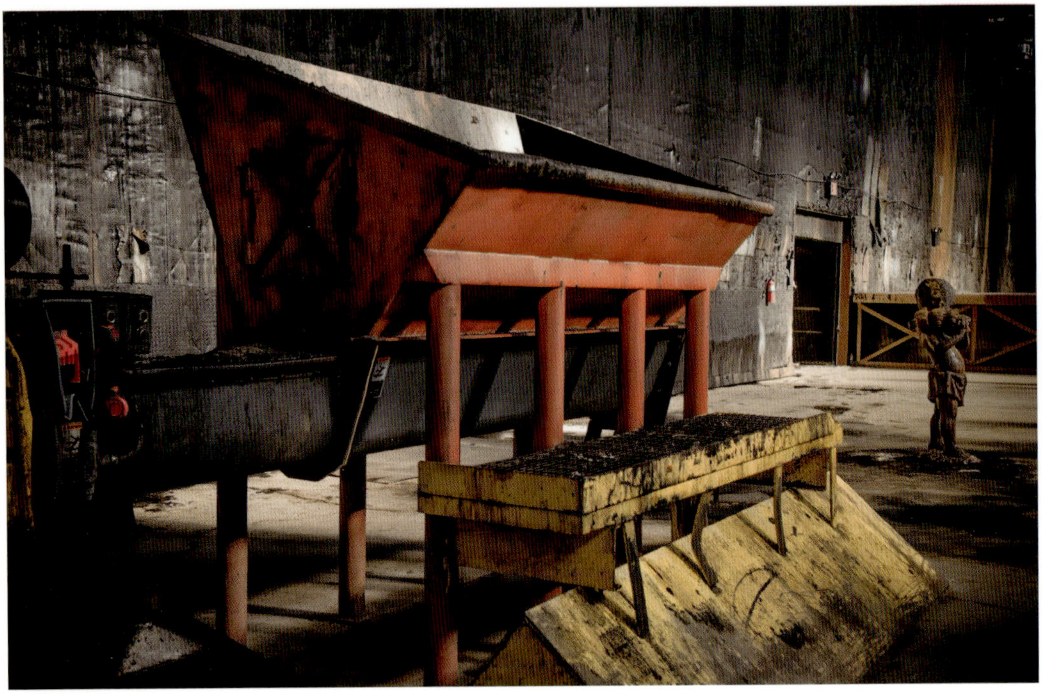

Machinery used in the sugar-refining process, and one of Kara Walker's sugar babies on the right. This sugar baby is carrying a load of bananas.

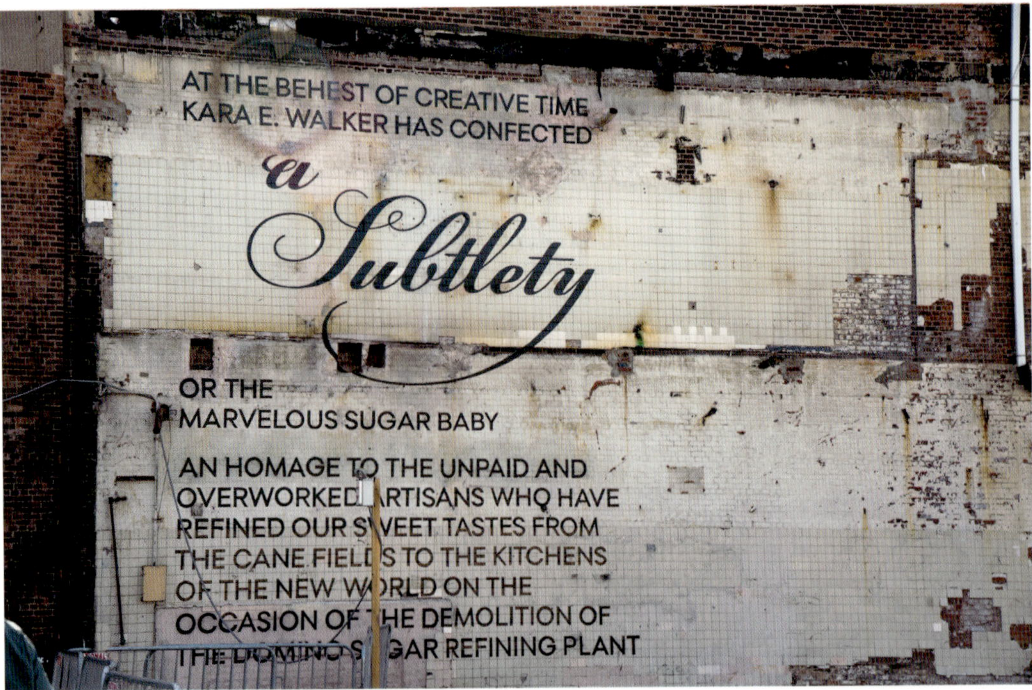

The sign on the wall of the factory notes: "A Subtlety" is an homage to the unpaid and overworked artisans who have refined our sweet tastes from the cane field to the kitchens of the new world on the occasion of the demolition of the Domino Sugar Refining Plant.

The centerpiece of "A Subtlety" is the enormous female sphinx, created from white sugar.

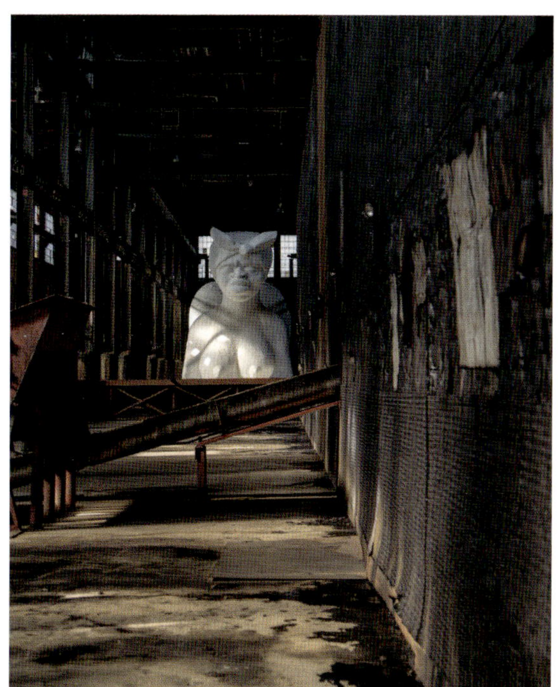

Also impressive are the basket-carrying children sculptures surrounding the sphinx. Most of the children sculptures are made of resin coated in molasses. The sugar from the molasses melted and pooled at the bottom and on parts of the figures.

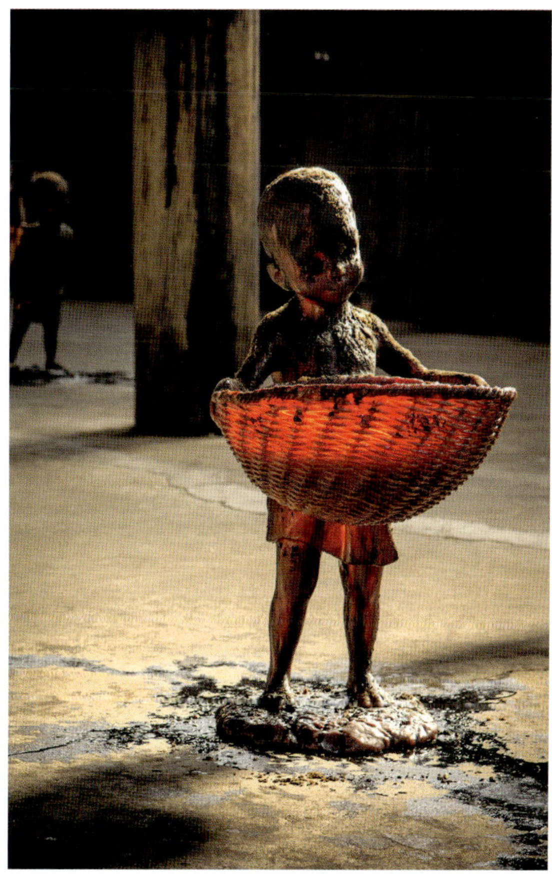

6

THE HIGH LINE

The High Line is an elevated park that occupies what was a former raised railway in the 1930s for freight trains making deliveries to the Meat Packing District and warehouses on the West Side of Manhattan. The High Line, one of New York's immensely popular urban attractions, is located on the West Side on Tenth Avenue and originally ran between Gansesvoort/14th and 20nd Streets, and section three was recently added to extend to 34th Street, ending at the new Hudson Yards. Trains ran directly through some buildings, making for easy distribution of goods. In the 1920s, grade level crossings became so dangerous that the city ordered all tracks to be elevated. Tenth Avenue was given the grizzly nickname "Death Avenue". Men on horses—the West Side Cowboys—soon rode in front of the trains waving red warning flags.

Due to the Eisenhower Highway Interstate System and increased trucking over the years, train traffic delivering goods to the West Side abated to near zero in the 1980s. New York residents started calling the tracks an eyesore and demanded they be razed. Mayor Rudy Giuliani signed the demolition order. Opposition to the High Line included these folks and real estate moguls who saw the line as in the way of future upward expansion. It was not to be.

The High Line was the brainchild of Joshua David and Robert Hammond. They met at a community-planning meeting in 1999, and soon founded Friends of the High Line. They loved the High Line's look of ruin and saw it as a new possibility to experience the city. They saw that grasses, trees, and wildflowers thrived on the high rail, and before the slated demolition could take place, David and Hammond decided the elevated tracks needed to stay. After many challenges, including legal ones, the groundbreaking finally occurred in April of 2006, and the first section opened three years later.

Friends of the High Line ran an ideas competition, and in doing so, drew awareness to the structure. Working with Mayor Bloomberg, designers, urban planners, architects, neighborhood associations, horticulturists, and local businesses, the Friends of High

Line fought until their dream was realized, in just ten years. The High Line is now one of the hottest tourist destinations in New York, and completely transformed the West Side from a slum to a bustling high-end district of town. New buildings going up adjacent to the High Line make the entire area very popular for visitors and residents alike. With the recent addition, the High Line runs for nearly one-and-a-half miles, and attracts roughly six million visitors per year in the twenty years since its opening, more than any other tourist site in New York. Hammond and David are, however, disappointed: they had envisioned the High Line as a community park to engage residents of Chelsea and the surrounding areas, and hope to attract more locals and residents of the two housing projects bookending the High Line. The High Line inspired other cities around the world to take on similar projects, including Atlanta, Philadelphia, and Dallas—it is a fantastic illustration of urban re-use of public lands.

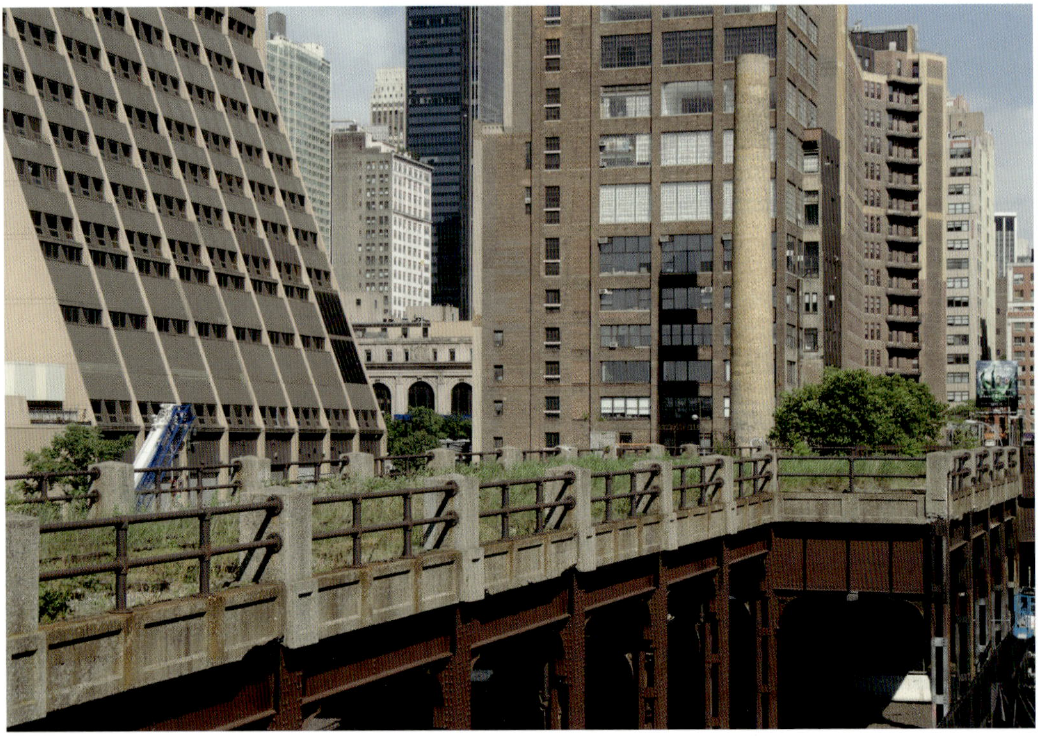

View of the High Line the West Side of Manhattan from one of the overlooks.

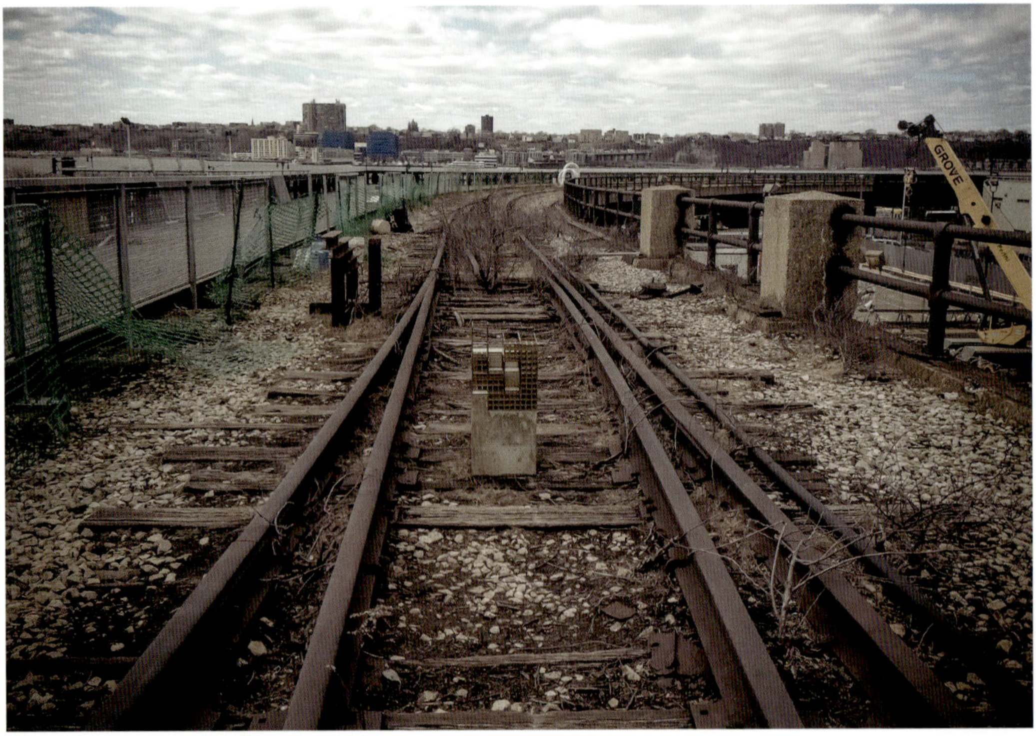

A view from the High Line pre-construction.

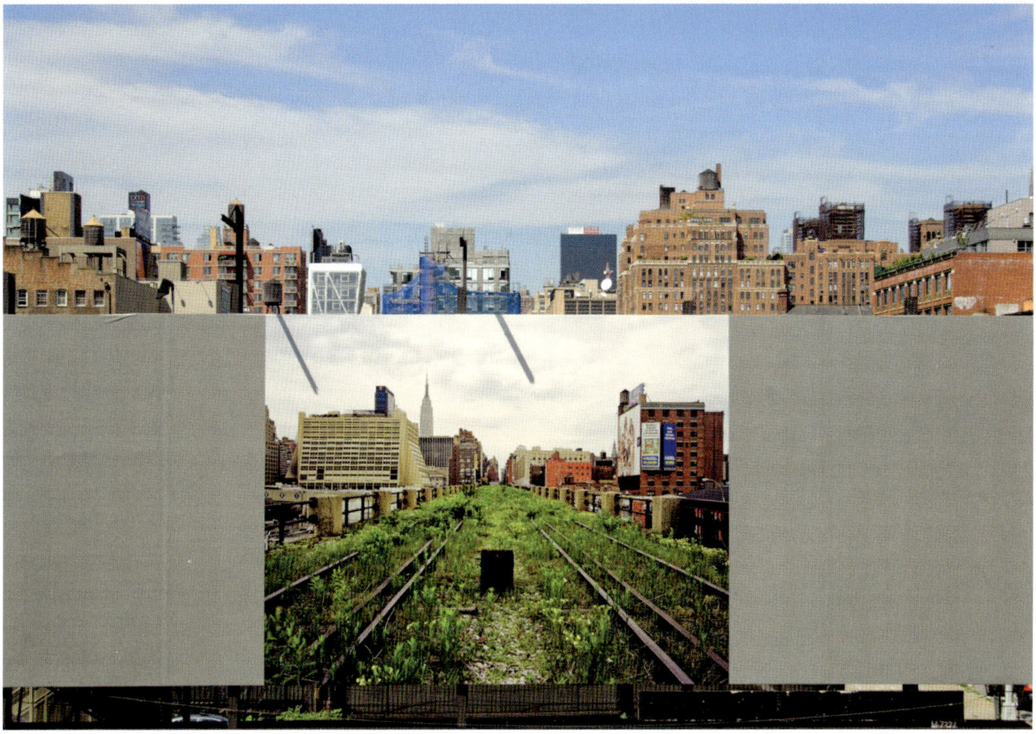

A billboard along the side of the High Line depicts what the tracks looked like before construction began.

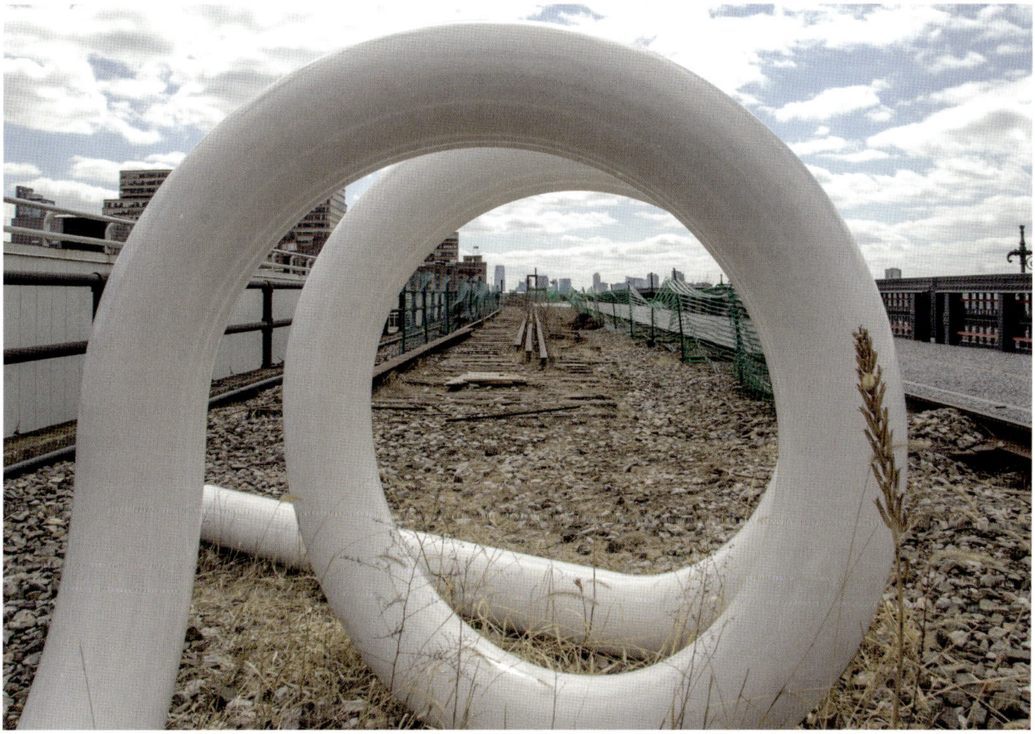

There were several early art installations along the High Line along the section between 30th and 34th Street.

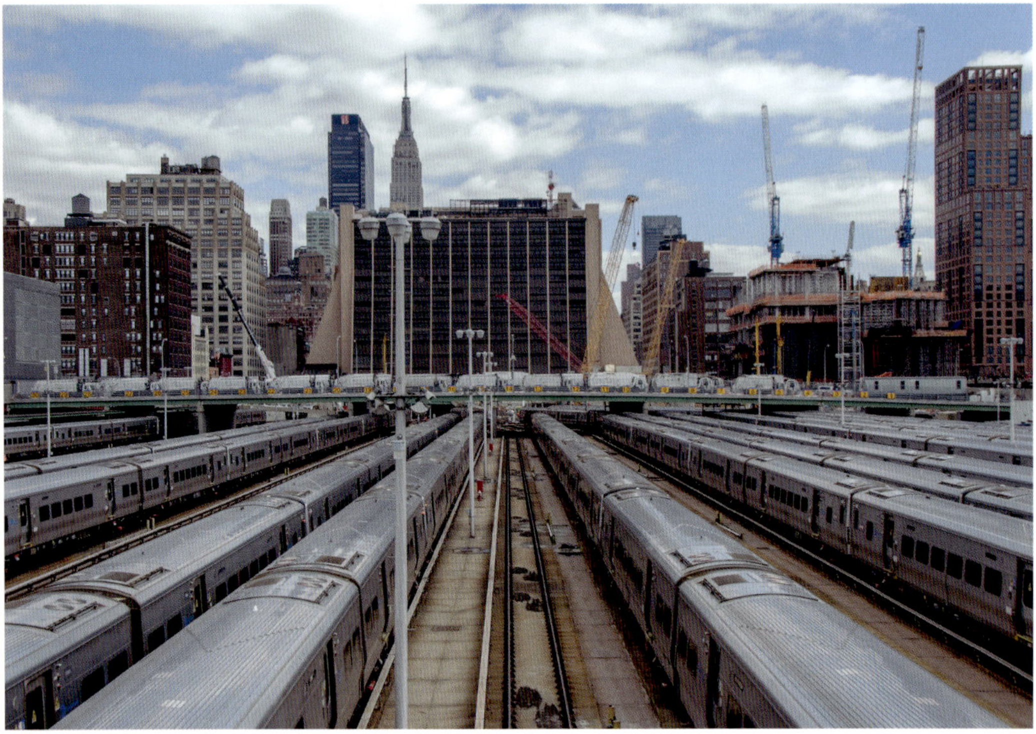

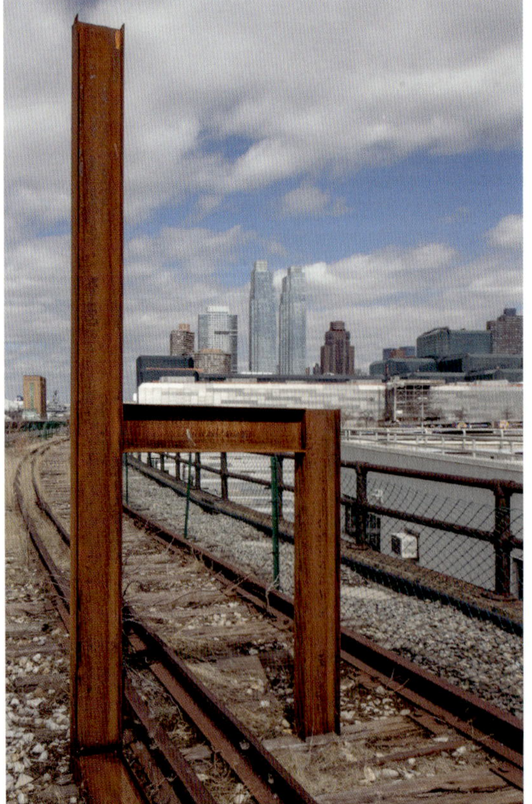

Above: View of the Long Island Rail Yard before it was partially covered to make way for the new Hudson Yards.

Left: Art installations appeared before construction started on the third section.

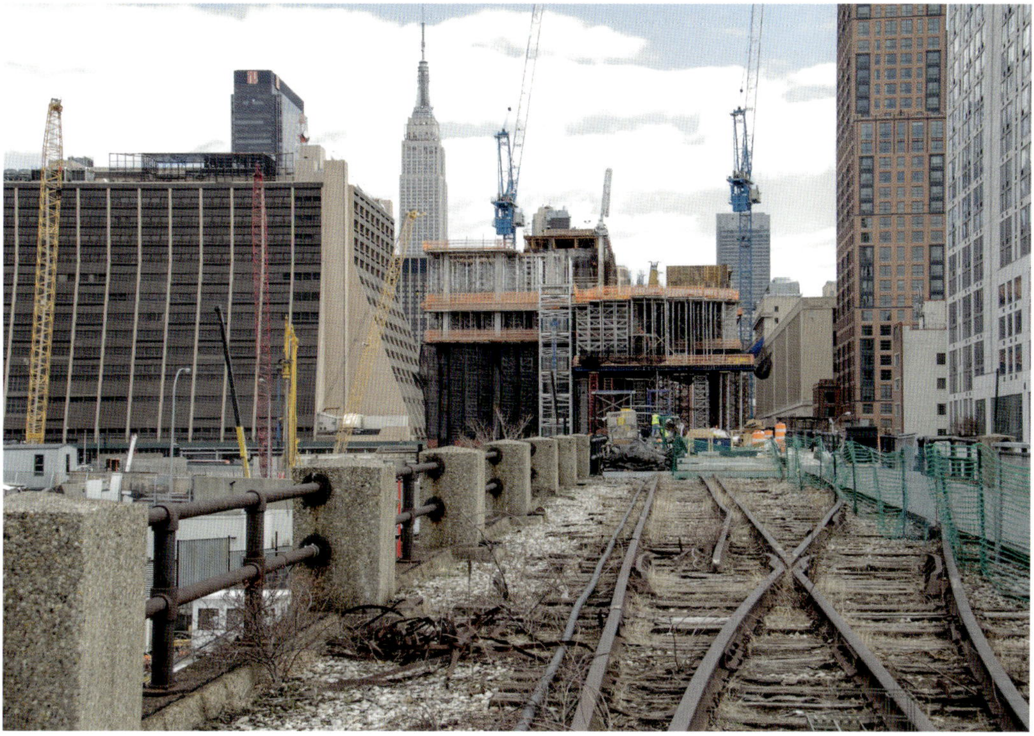

Above: This is a look at Section three of the pre-construction High Line, which opened in 2014.

Right: Vegetation grows quite well on the High Line. The Empire State Building is seen in the background.

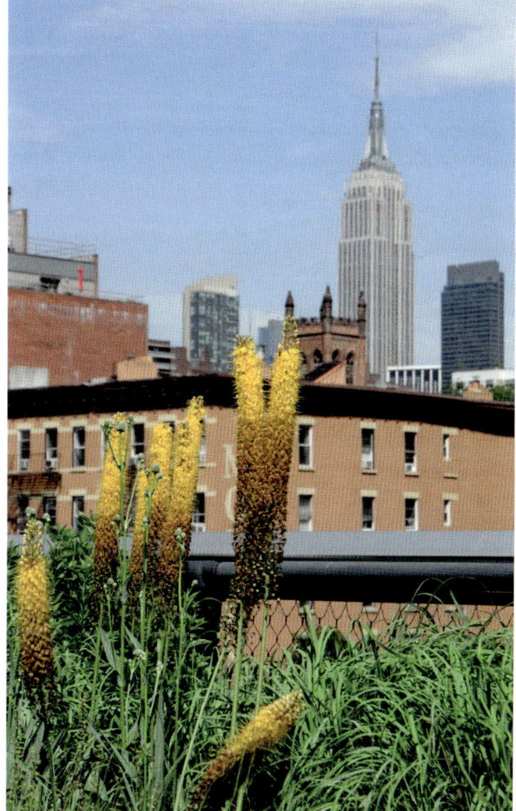

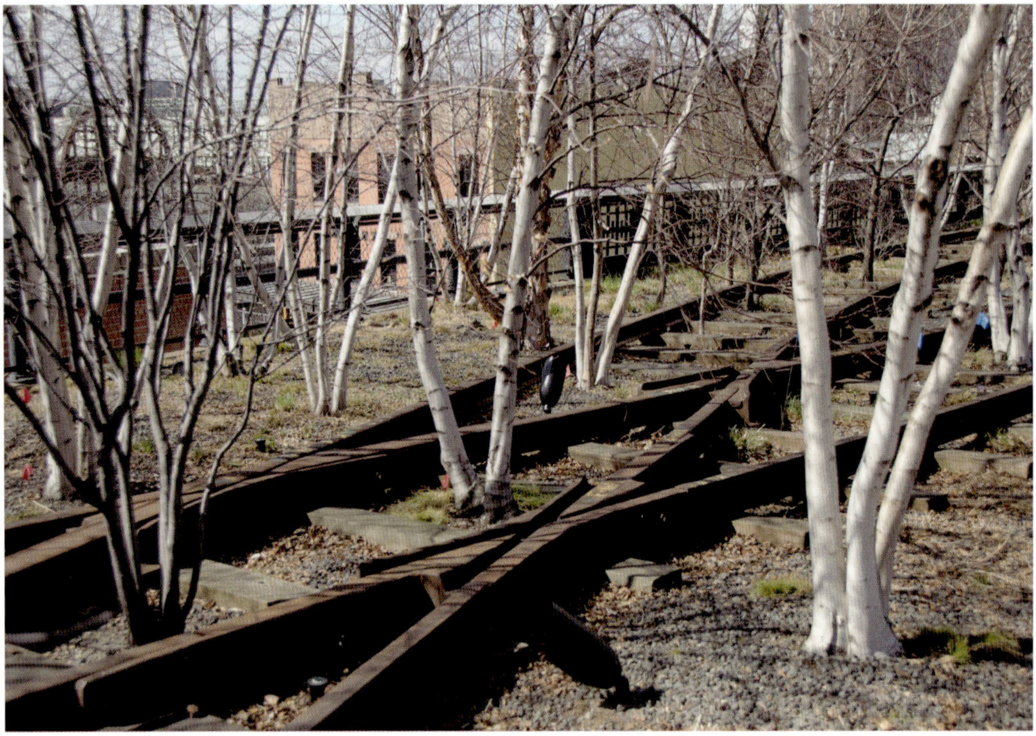

Birch trees are thriving on top of the High Line.

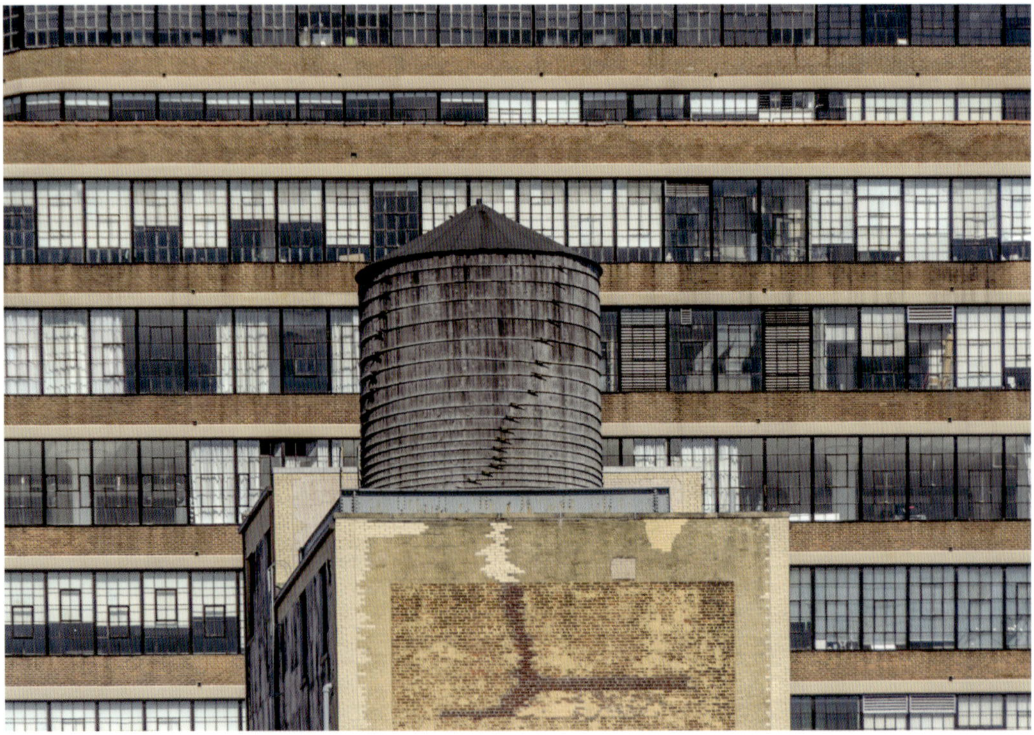

One of the buildings one walks past while strolling along the High Line.

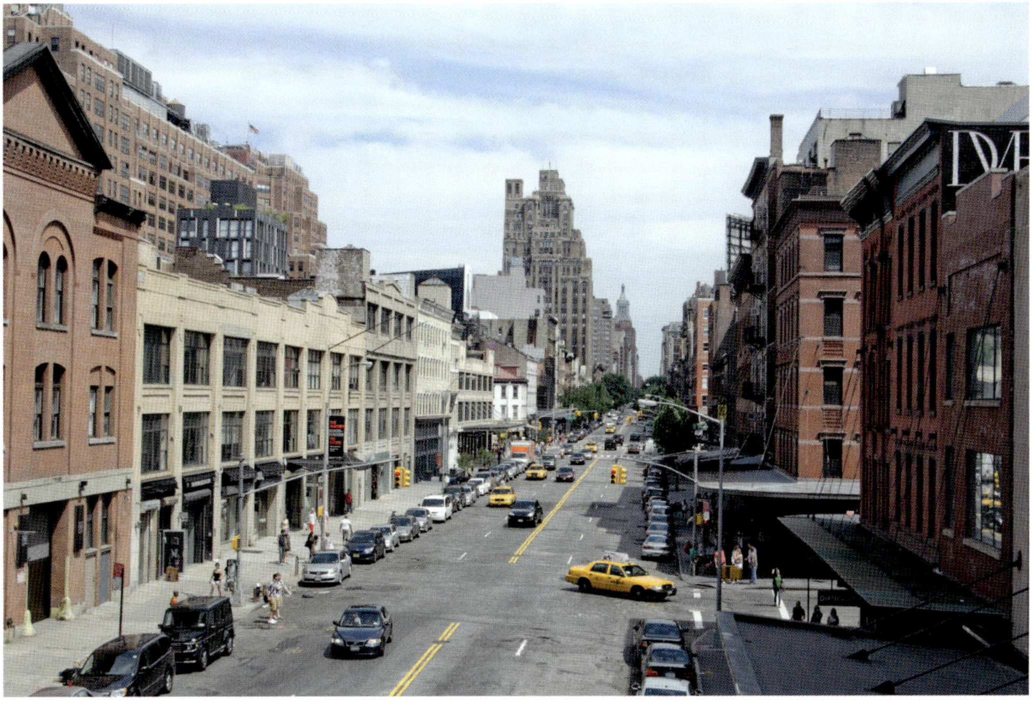

A view looking east on 14th St.

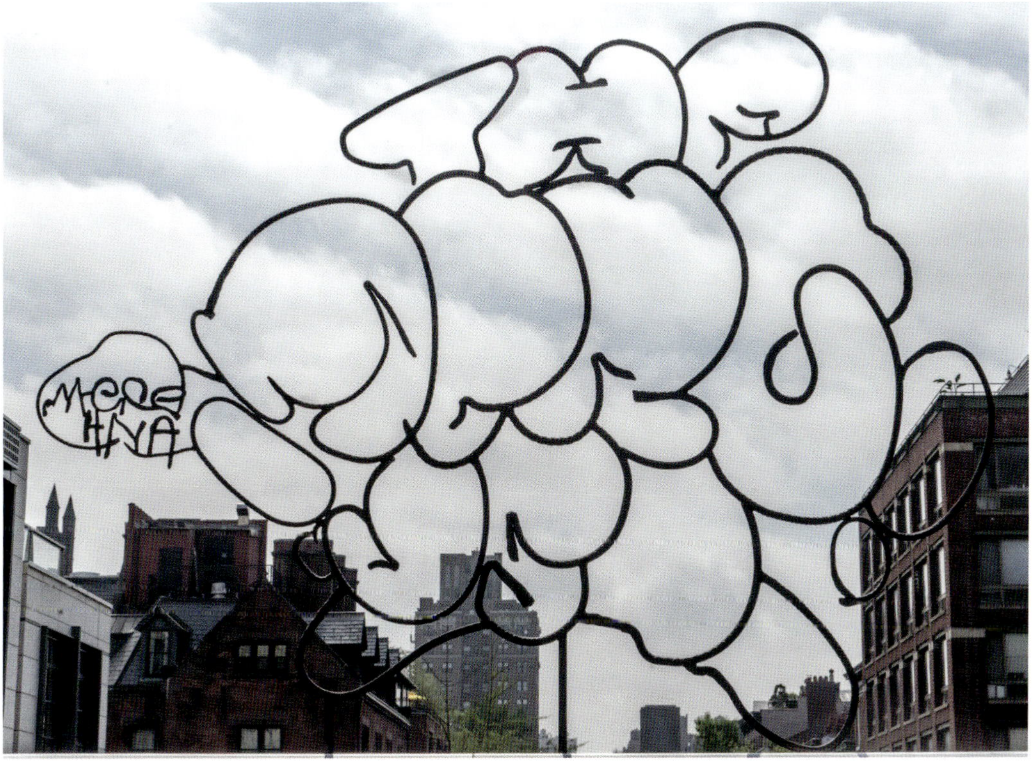

An art installation along the High Line is a rusty iron version of graffiti.

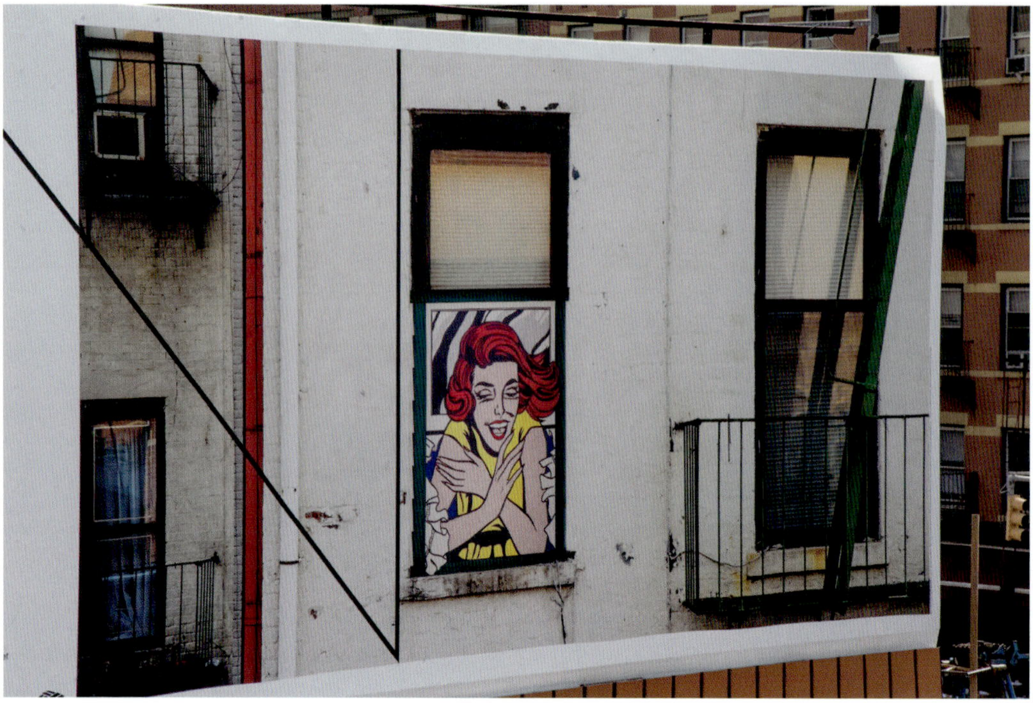

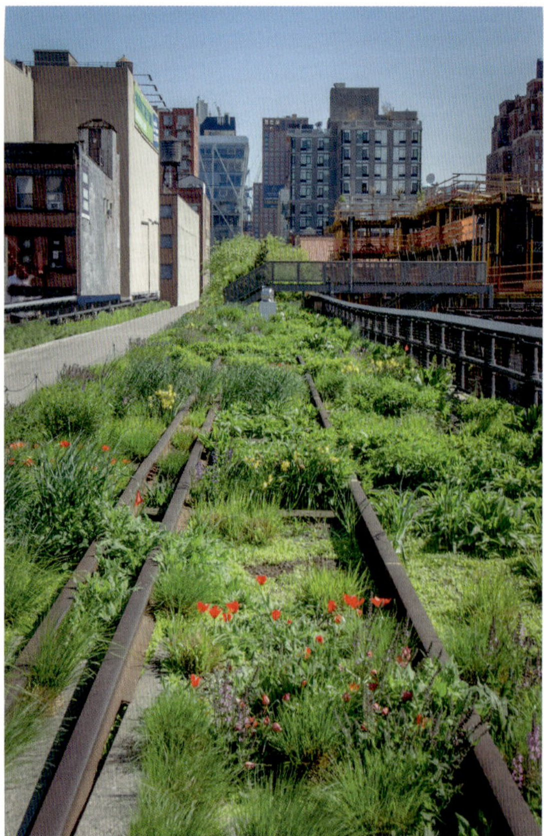

Above: Apartment dwellers along the High Line have a sense of humor, a necessity given the proximity to the buildings, which in some cases are mere feet away.

Left: The High Line before construction.

7

ELLIS ISLAND, THE ISLAND OF TEARS

The hairs on the back of my neck stood up as I walked into the main hall at Ellis Island. In my mind's eye, I could see the immigrants waiting in line; I could sense their apprehension. The immigrants just arrived from Europe on a stressful voyage in the third class or steerage section. Unfairly, first and second-class passengers are examined on the ship and allowed to disembark in Manhattan; steerage and third class must take a ferry to Ellis Island for examination. None of the immigrants know what is going to happen to them and most do not speak English. They wait in line for doctors to poke them and look at their scalp for favus, in their eyes for trachoma. Sometimes a chalk mark will be drawn on them. The place is packed with other immigrants speaking in different foreign languages. It smells like sweat and body odor and wet wool. They are nervous and exhausted, with frightened children clinging to them.

The majestic Registry Room was empty the day I was there, a rare event indeed. Ellis Island had just been hit by Hurricane Sandy and was closed to the public. I was there to document the damage as a FEMA photographer, and I witnessed significant destruction.

I can only imagine what the experience of immigration was like, being processed through Ellis Island. Exciting yet terrifying at the same time? At the height of migration to the U.S., around 1907, Ellis Island processed over 10,000 immigrants every day. The immigrants came to escape famine, they came for work, they came because they were persecuted, they came for love, they came for a better life. Some 12-million immigrants processed through Ellis Island between January 2, 1892, and November 12, 1954, when it closed.

Before an immigrant boarded a ship in their home country, they needed to prove they would not become indigent, were not an "idiot" or insane, were relatively healthy, and could get a job. Many immigrants had families or sponsors in the United States that would provide employment. The ship companies were required to pay for immigrants' return passage if the United States rejected the immigrants for admission; accordingly, the ship companies ensured these rules were followed. The deportation rate at Ellis Island was around 2%.

Imagine being one of these immigrants: Doctors observed you for signs of lameness or deformities as you ascended the stairs to the 2nd floor for processing. As you were examined by a doctor in the Registry Room, if you were unfortunate enough to have a chalk mark drawn on you, you were then sent to a new line where another doctor further examined you. From there, the doctors either deported or ushered you to the hospital complex. You could be sent over to the hospital for any number of reasons. When the doctors looked in your eyes, trachoma may be evident. Trachoma is a highly contagious bacterial disease that causes blindness if it is gone untreated (today, it can be cured with simple antibiotics). The handling of trachoma at Ellis Island hospital was to scrub the insides of the eyelids twice a day with a wire brush. Most people with trachoma were deported; the United States did not want people who might go blind and enter the welfare system. Immigration was for the healthy and able-bodied.

You, as an immigrant, may need to be quarantined for being in proximity to scarlet fever, though you were not sick. (Many immigrants died from scarlet fever, whether on the ship or while in quarantine.) The experience must have been a very frustrating time for the patients, who gazed out the window at the Statue of Liberty and Manhattan across the Hudson River.

In addition to all the other activities vying for immigrants' attention, there were many unscrupulous characters awaiting them at Ellis Island: inspectors who would take bribes for the promise of entry, cheating money exchangers, and men who allowed entrance for young women in exchange for certain promises. Eventually, employees were fired for these practices, and that quickly ended these shenanigans. Immigration was not as bad as it sounds, however; there were also aid groups helping steer an immigrant through the process, including the YMCA, Travellers' Aid, the Hebrew Immigrant Aid Society, and the Salvation Army. In reality, the process for most immigrants took only a few hours and required no paperwork.

1902 saw the construction of the hospital complex. Landfill excavated from the new subway system being constructed on Manhattan was imported to Ellis Island in order to enlarge the island. Channels were dredged and docks constructed. The first hospital buildings on the island burned after a mere four years, and new fireproof buildings were built. The hospital wards were state-of-the-art. The buildings have no square corners; even the intersection of the ceilings and walls are rounded. During this period, not much was known about how diseases are transmitted, and many thought that germs would collect in the square corners. As one walked down a hallway, the wards with the most ill patients were at the end of the corridor, to avoid having staff and patients walk past these wards constantly. Not a lot was understood about these illnesses then, because antibiotics had not yet been discovered. It has been reported, however, that not a single nurse got sick while treating patients at Ellis.

The hospital at Ellis Island closed in 1930 due in part to a downturn in immigration after WWI. After this time, the FBI used the facility as a field office. Later the site became a military hospital. The military used the hospital for personnel suffering from post-traumatic stress disorder. In 1954 the complex was abandoned.

During the hospital's lifespan, 10,000 patients from seventy-five countries were treated at the Ellis Island hospital complex. During that time, over 3,500 immigrants died there, half of them children, and 350 babies were born. Babies born on Ellis Island had no guarantee of U.S. citizenship. Ellis Island has often been referred to as the Island of Tears; many hospitalized people understood that they might never get off the island to step on actual U.S. soil. Today, one can visit Ellis Island and visit the museum and Registry Room to view the inspectors' records for their ancestors' names and ship names.

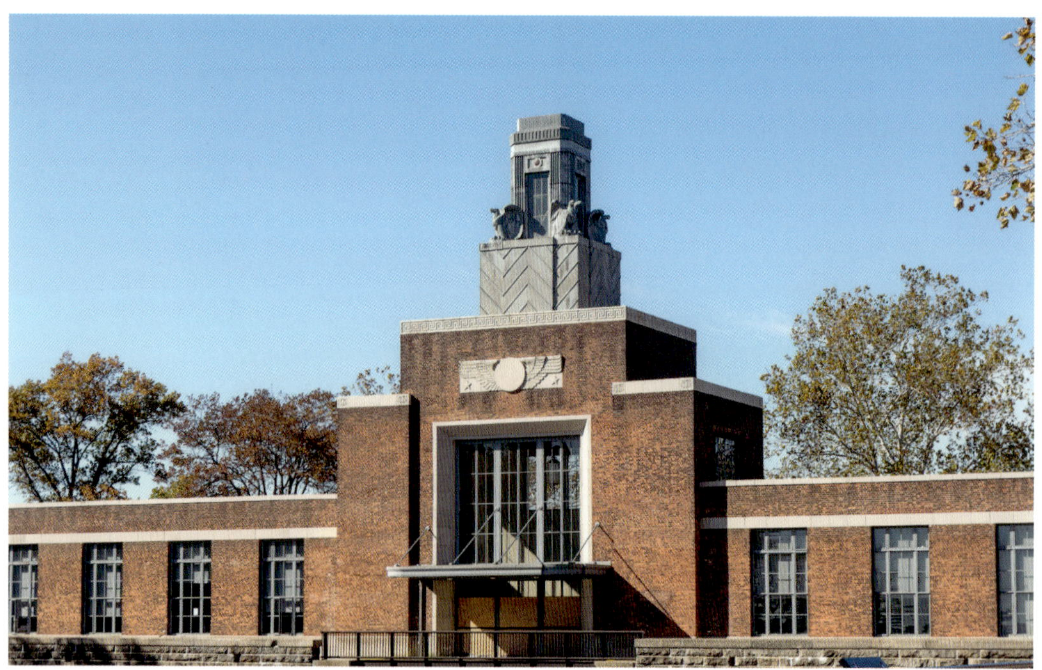

The distinctively Art Deco ferry building at Ellis Island was added on in 1936. Four bronze eagles flank the top squarish cupola. Accepted immigrants would go here after processing to catch a ferry to leave Ellis Island.

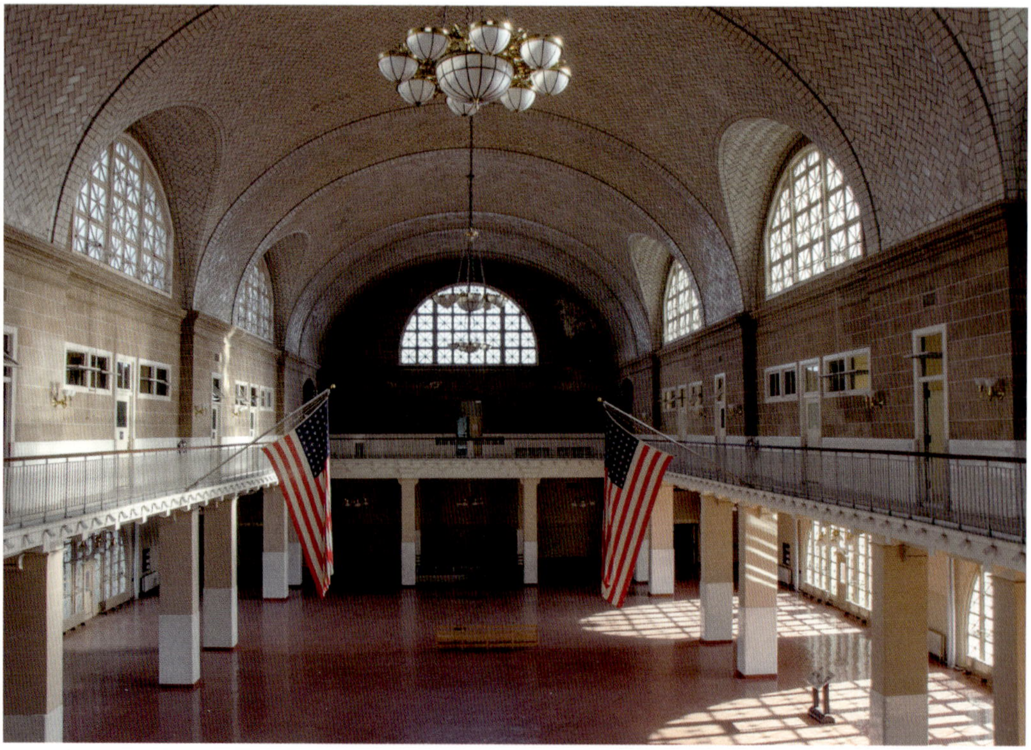

Ellis Island, which houses the Immigration Museum, was heavily damaged from Hurricane Sandy in October 2012. This photograph shows the Registry Room where immigrants entered the United States to be processed.

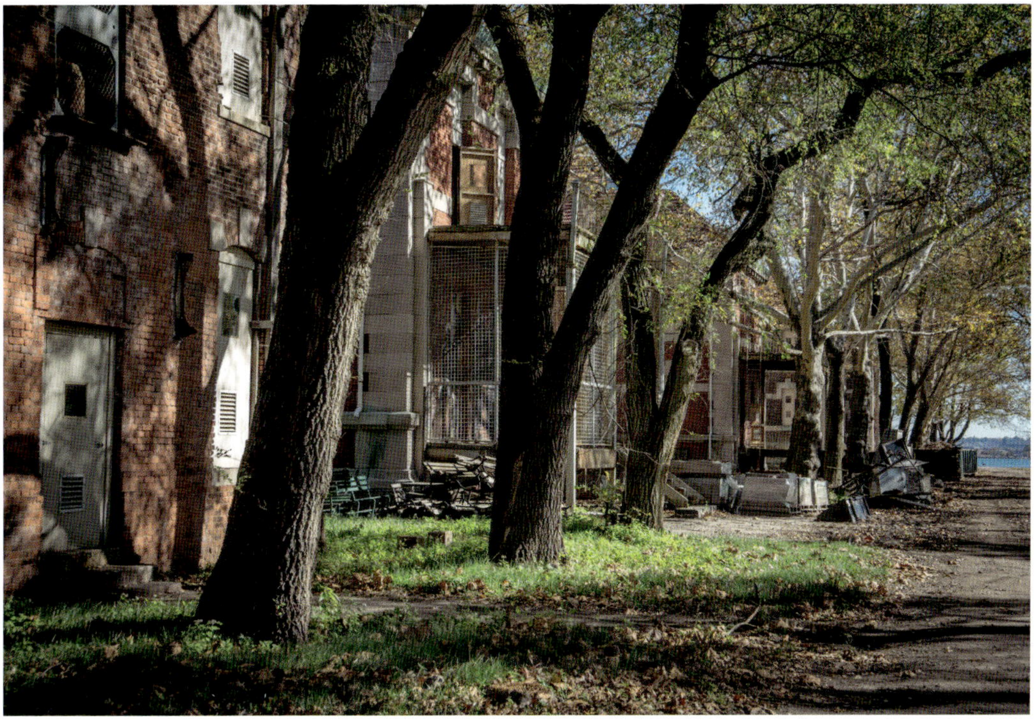

Above: The south side of Ellis Island contains the twenty-nine buildings that made up the hospital complex.

Left: Some of the words of immigrants scribbled on walls have been preserved and are on view at Ellis Island.

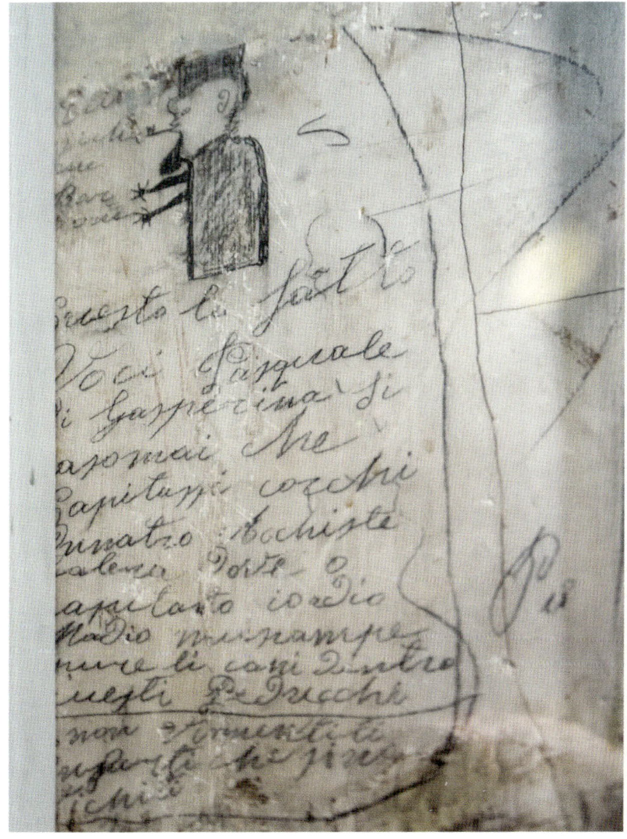

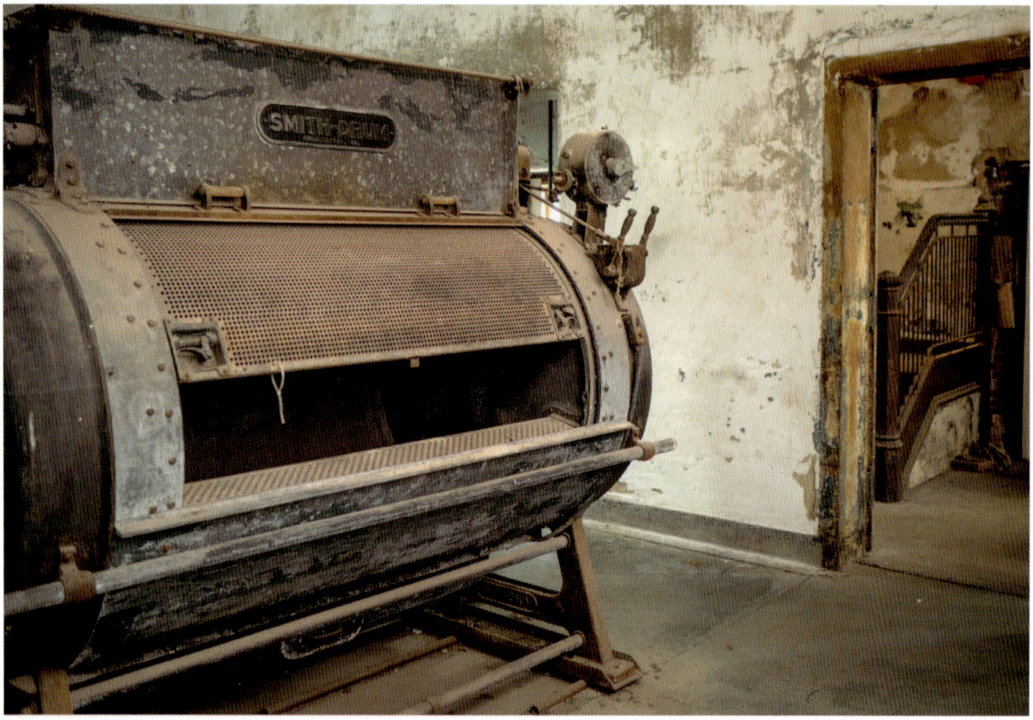

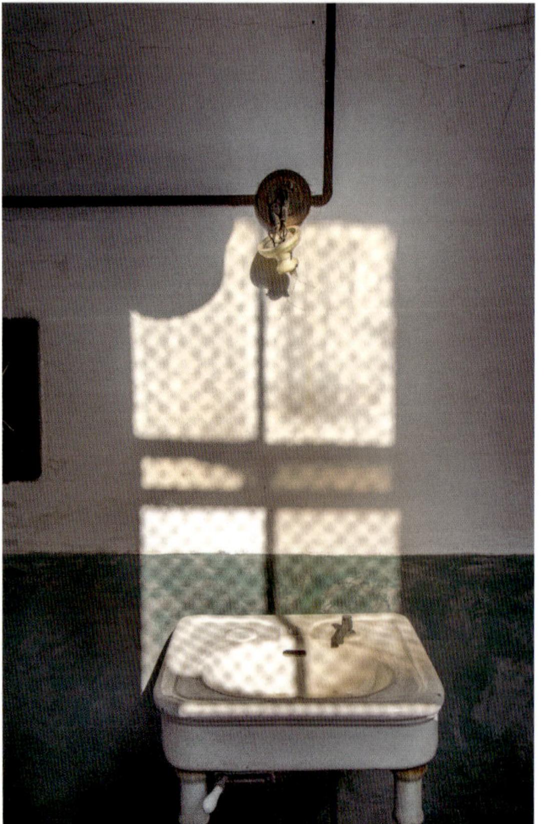

Above: A machine in the laundry room of the hospital complex.

Left: Infectious disease wards contained two sinks each: one for washing hands and one for spitting.

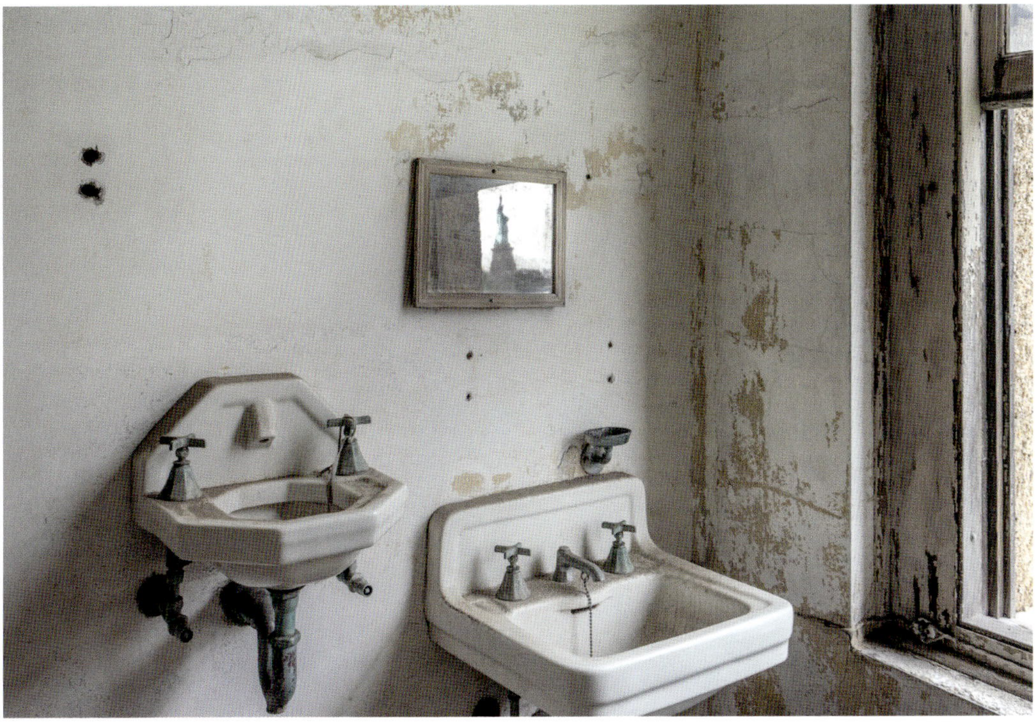

Above: A mirror in the bathroom in one of the hospital wards reflects what so many immigrants had yet to see up close: The Statue of Liberty.

Right: The ceiling and the corners are rounded in this hospital ward to prevent germs from collecting in the corner.

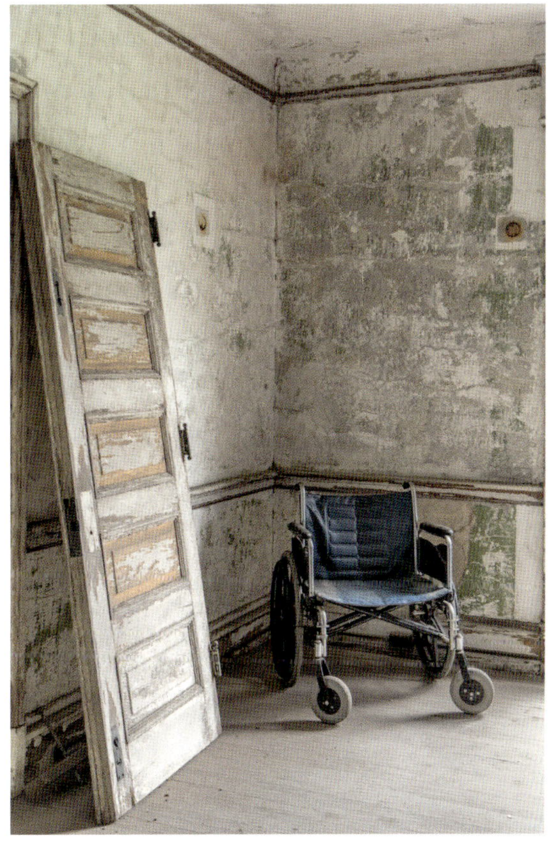

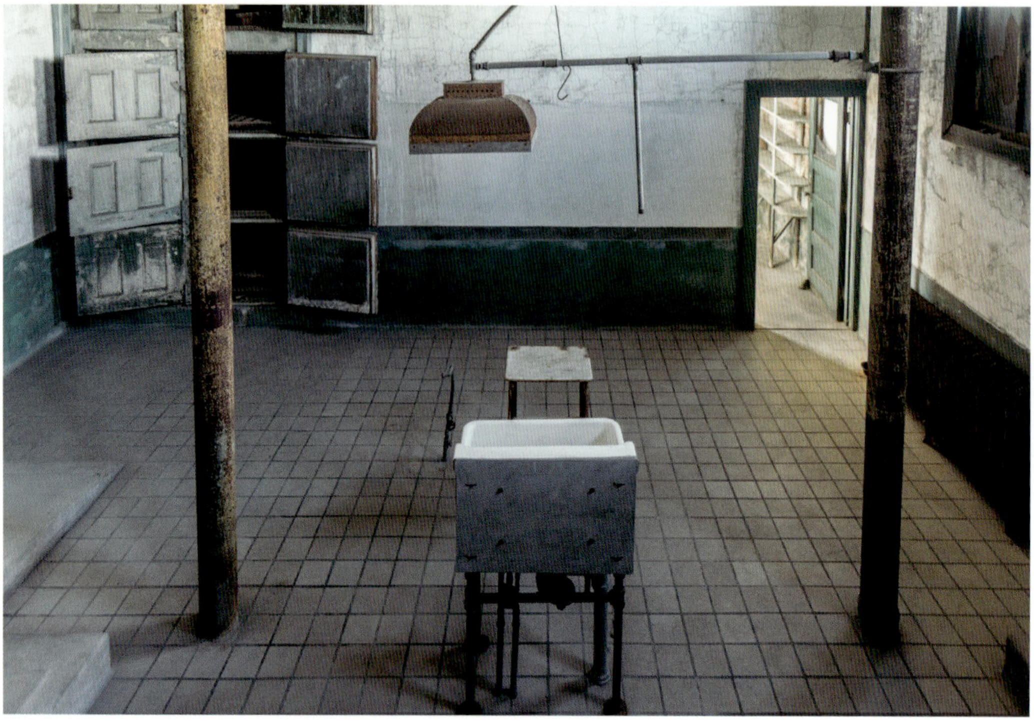

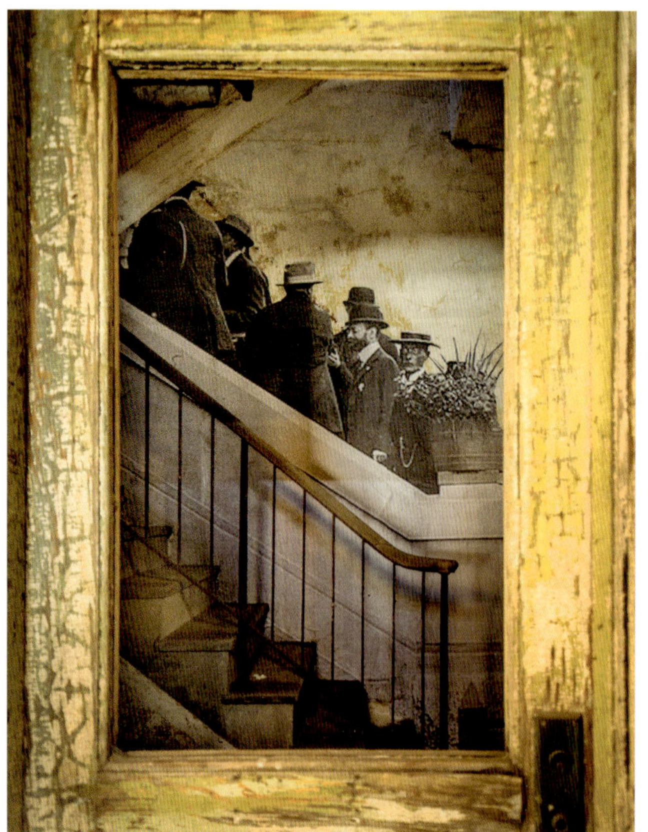

Above: The morgue had compartments for eight bodies and a viewing platform for medical students and interested doctors.

Left: Artist JR created an art installation at the hospital in 2105 entitled *Unframed - Ellis Island* to draw attention to and raise money for Save Ellis Island, a non-profit that is helping restore Ellis Island.

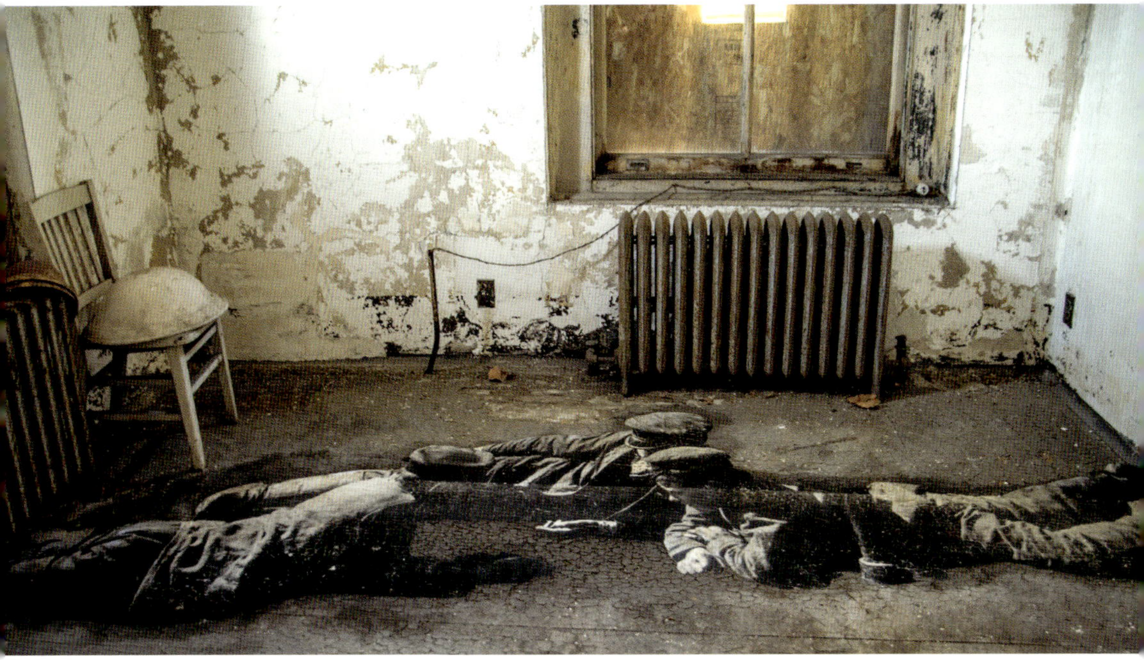

Above: JR's installation features huge photographs of immigrants, doctors and nurses superimposed on plaster walls, wood, floors, lockers, etc., that allow the texture to bleed through. The photographs are designed to deteriorate over time. According to JR, the work will remain up "until it decides to disappear."

Right: Vines on a hospital window grow wild as the building deteriorates in the elements.

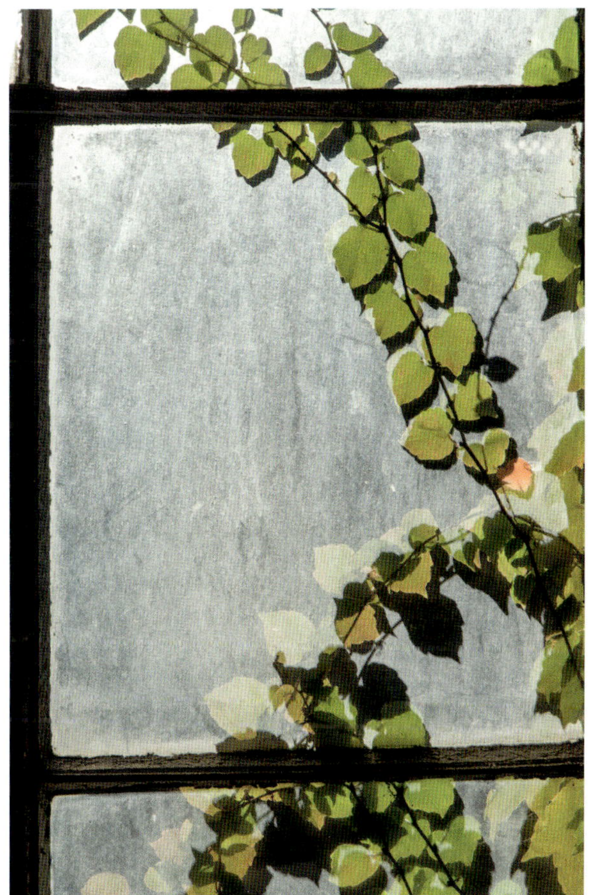

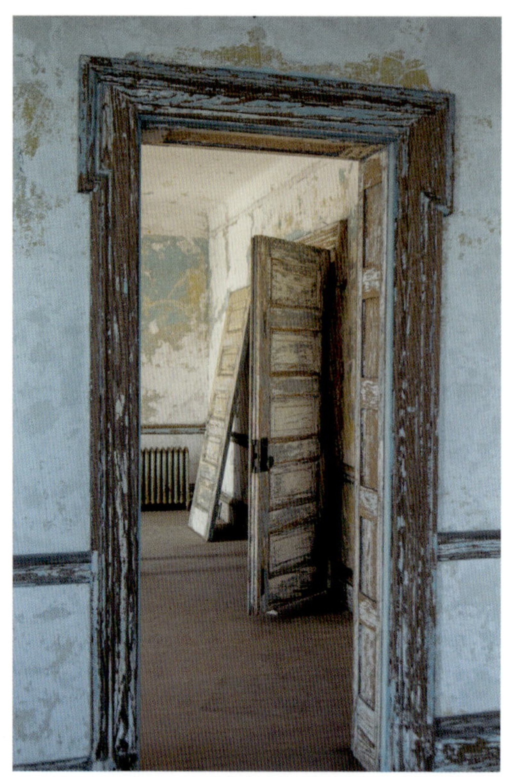

Left: The head doctor at Ellis Island received his own quarters, located on the second floor of one of the hospital buildings. The Public Health and Marine Hospital Service employed all the hospital's doctors.

Below: This photograph shows part of the steam heating system from the hospital complex at Ellis Island.

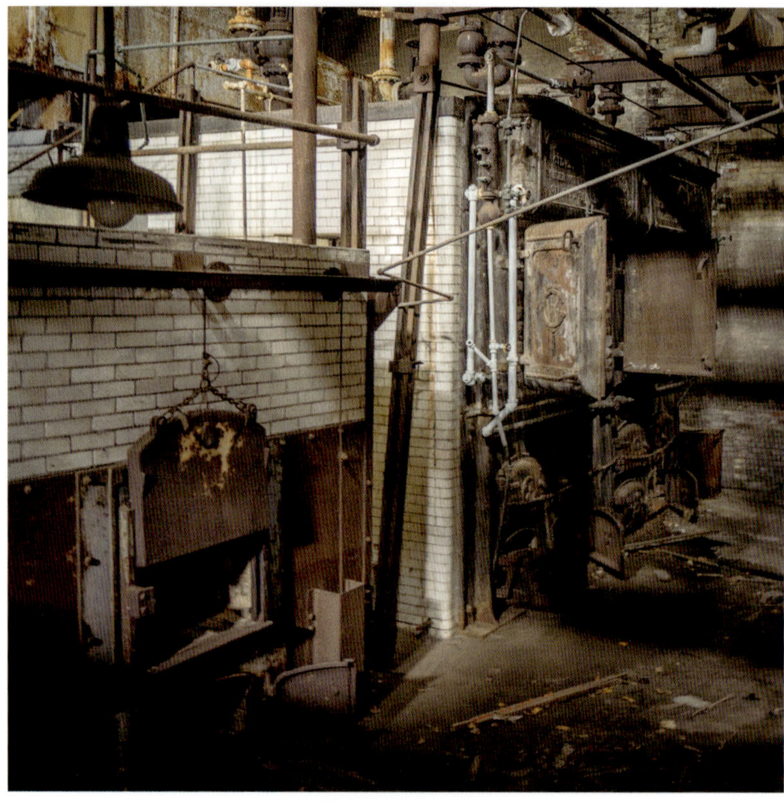

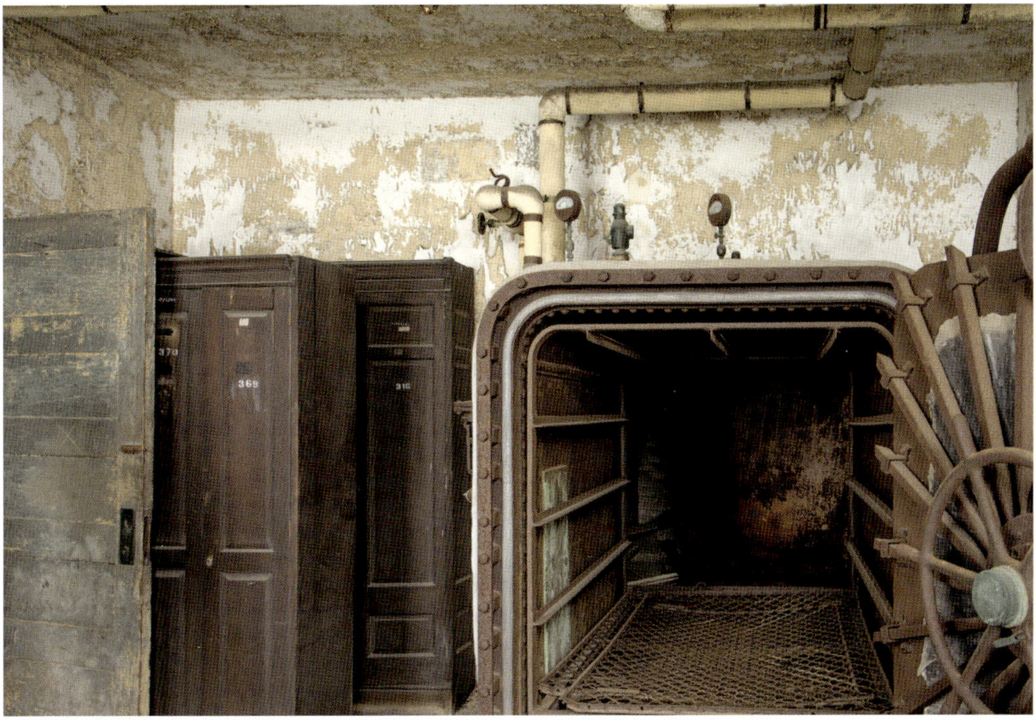

Above: A large autoclave for disinfecting mattresses sits in the hospital at Ellis Island.

Right: A bathroom in one of the wards at the Ellis Island hospital complex.

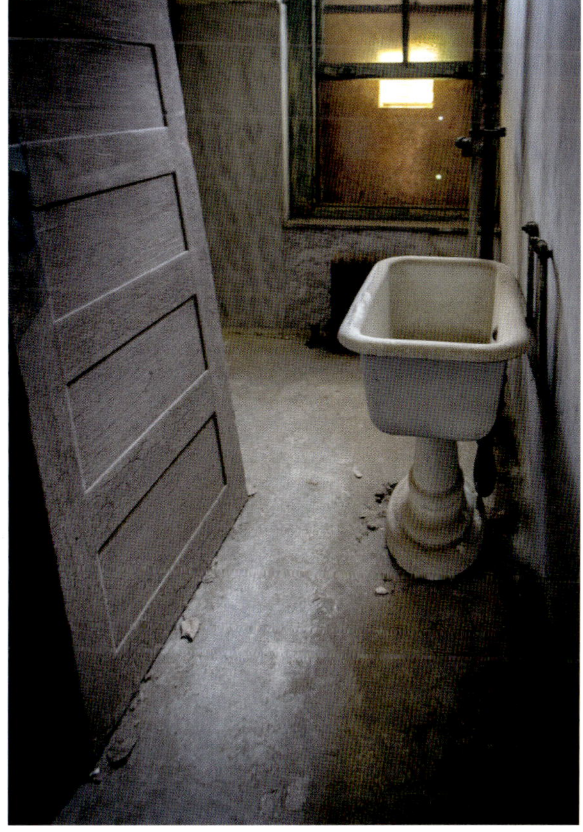

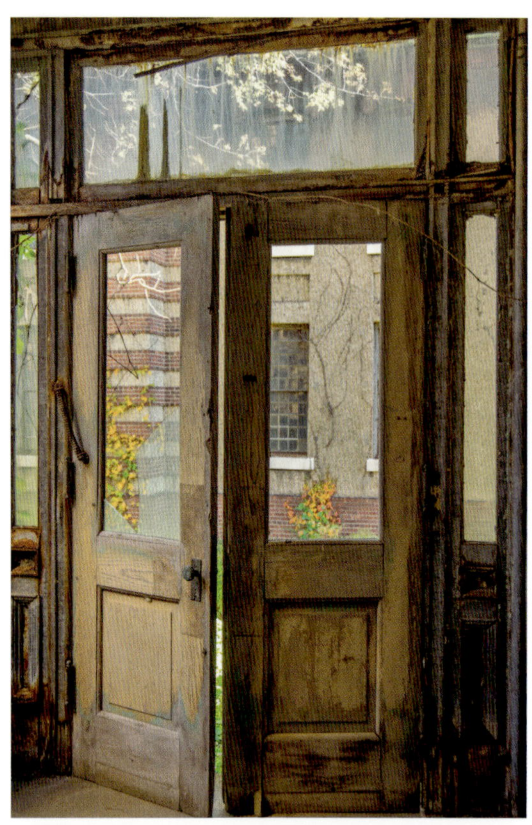

Left: Doors lead out to an autumn courtyard in the hospital.

Below: The exterior of some of the hospital buildings look across the Hudson River at lower Manhattan.

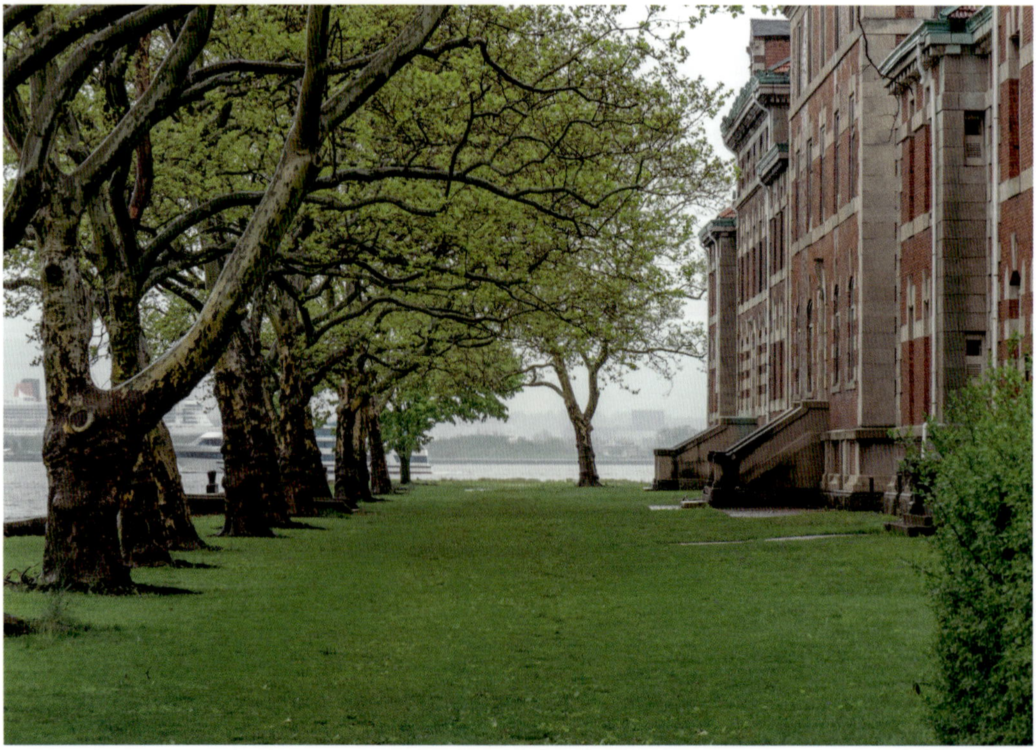

8

BLACKWELL'S ISLAND

Years ago, New York stashed its residents who were deemed unfit to live in civilized society, either because of insanity or smallpox, on an island in the East River named Blackwell's, known today as Roosevelt Island. The Asylum of the Insane, located on Blackwell's, was an institution full of abject horrors; if in doubt, just read Nelly Bly's book *Ten Days in a Madhouse*. Journalist Bly had herself institutionalized at Blackwell Island's insane asylum by "acting crazy" at a women's boarding house in New York City in the late 1880s (It was so easy to be committed at the time!). Bly was a reporter for the *New York World* and wanted to write about the conditions in the asylum via first-hand experience. After a few days, Bly identified her true identity and profession, but the doctors did not believe her and would not release her. Finally, the *World* editors rescued Bly. The ensuing story Bly wrote was so powerful with tales of abuse at the asylum that the authorities closed the institution. Remaining on the island is a large octagon that was originally the entrance to the asylum. The structures have been repurposed as apartments that opened in 2006, but the ghosts of patients may still linger on.

On the other end of the island, the ruins of the Renwick Smallpox Hospital still stand. Designed by James Renwick Jr. and built in the Gothic style in 1856, the hospital kept smallpox infected patients far away from the general population of New York. The hospital treated roughly 7,000 patients a year. Even though a vaccine was available, smallpox outbreaks in New York were common due to the large number if immigrants infected with the disease. Smallpox, a highly infectious virus, was eradicated from the planet by 1979 (although bioterrorism is still a consideration to some), and the building became obsolete. Abandoned in 1973, the building fell into greater disrepair. The Landmarks Preservation Commission and the City of New York initiated stabilization efforts, leaving the remains crumbling in a state of arrested decay. The remains consist mainly of the outer walls and a few dwindling staircases.

Access to the island is limited to busses and cars via the Queensboro Bridge, or for foot traffic, a tramway from Manhattan Island. A subway station (F Line) was installed in 1989. There is also a new NYC Ferry stop as well, which is certainly worth the $2.75 price tag. A local bus goes around the small island for twenty-five cents per ride.

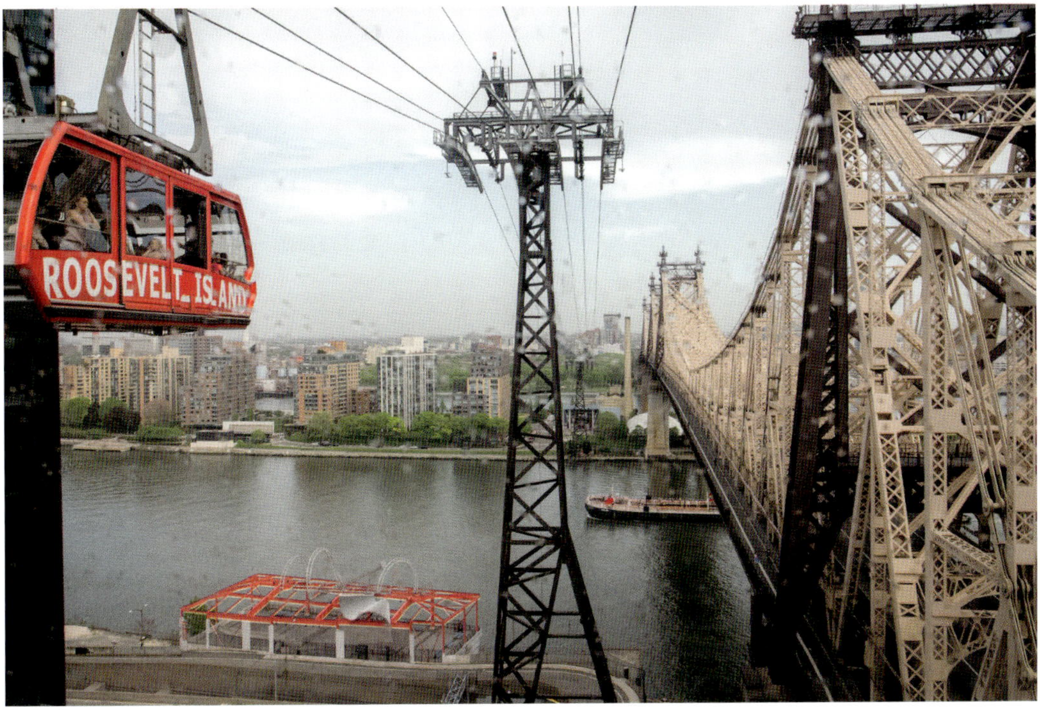

The best (and most scenic) way to get to Roosevelt Island is the MTA Tramway. It's quite a bargain for the price of a single subway ride.

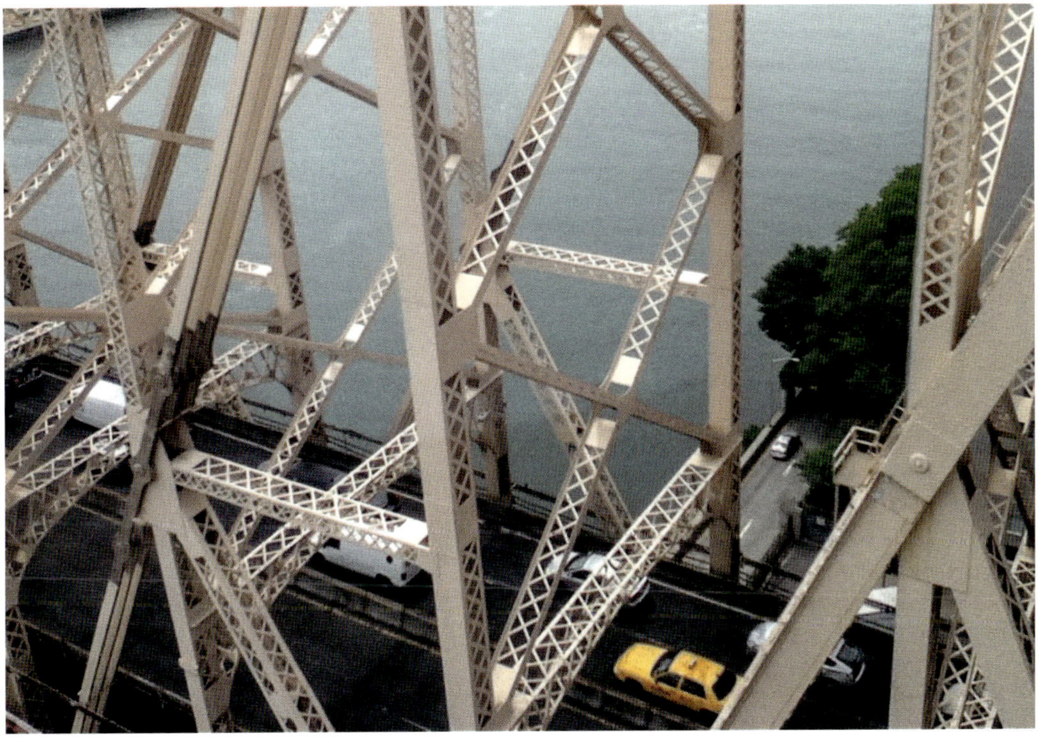

View from the Roosevelt Island Tramway, which runs parallel to the Queensboro Bridge across the East River.

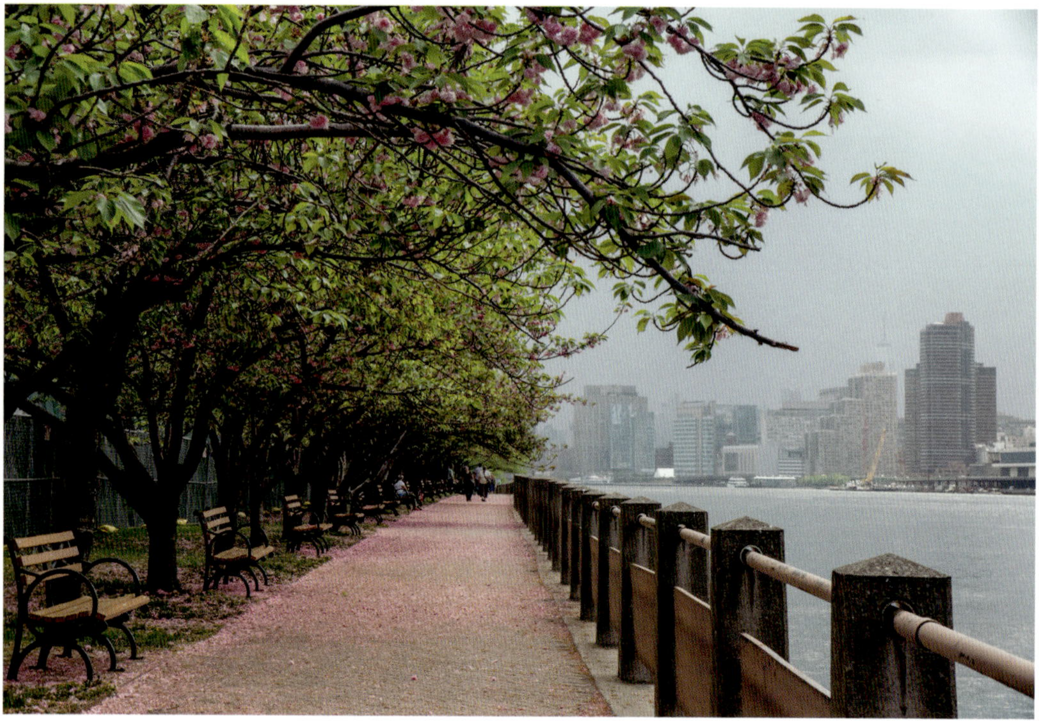

Renwick Smallpox Hospital is located on what was known as Blackwell's Island at that time.

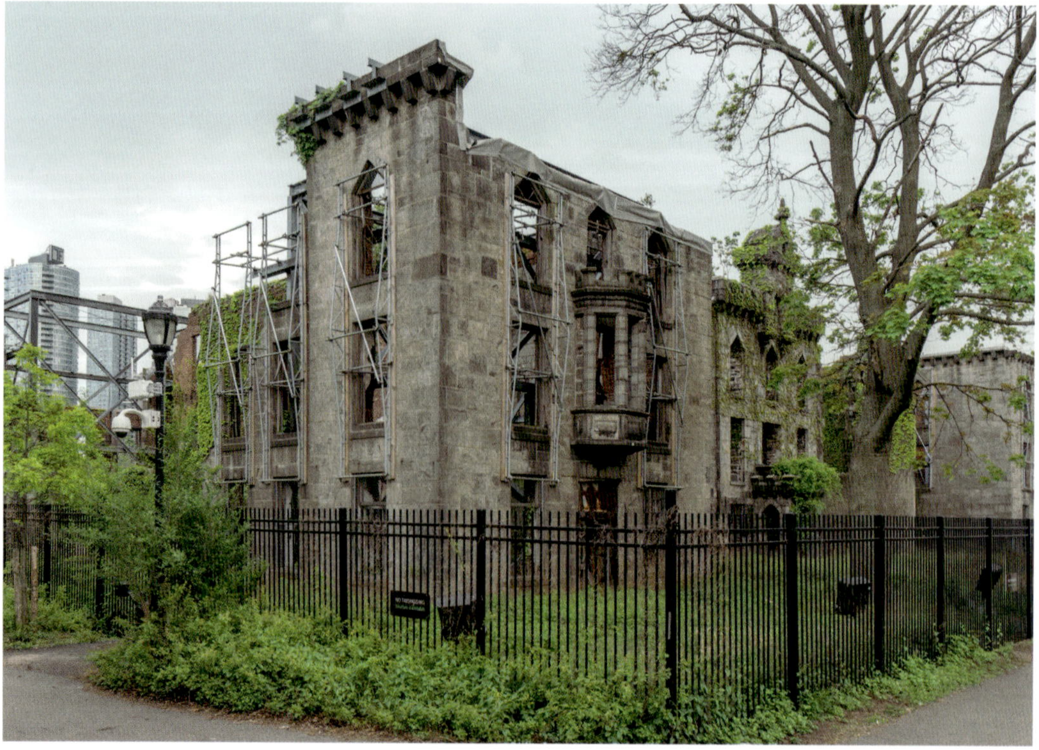

Remnants of the Renwick Smallpox Hospital on Roosevelt Island.

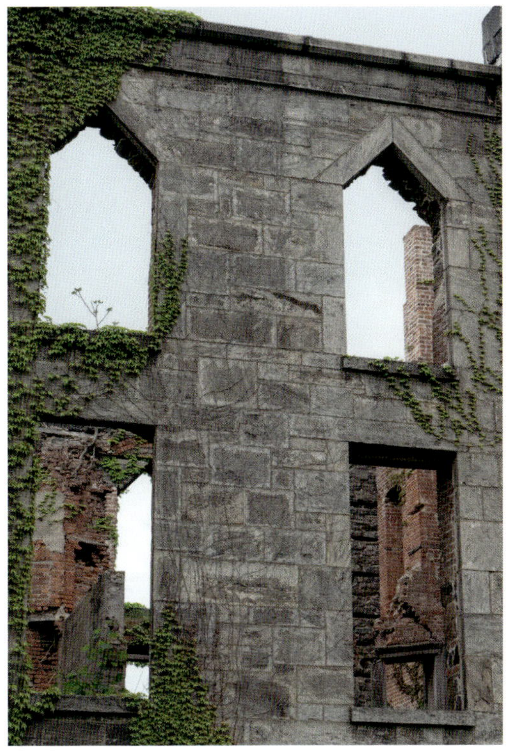

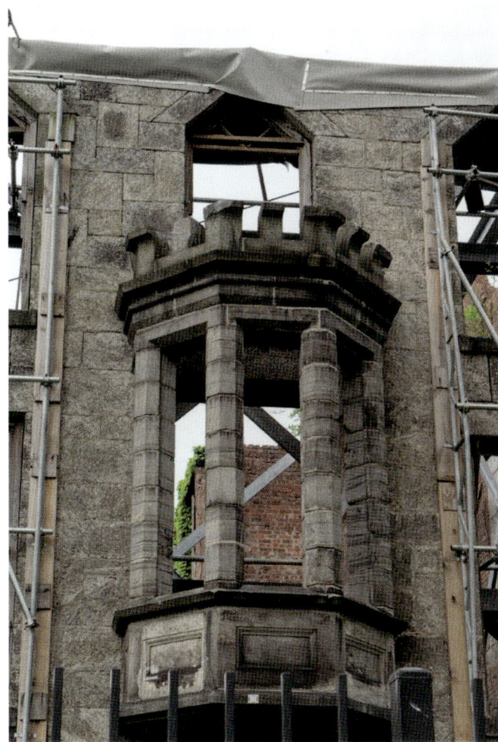

Left: The hospital was designed by James Renwick Jr. and was constructed with granite veneer blocks.

Right: The front of the building contained a large oriel window.

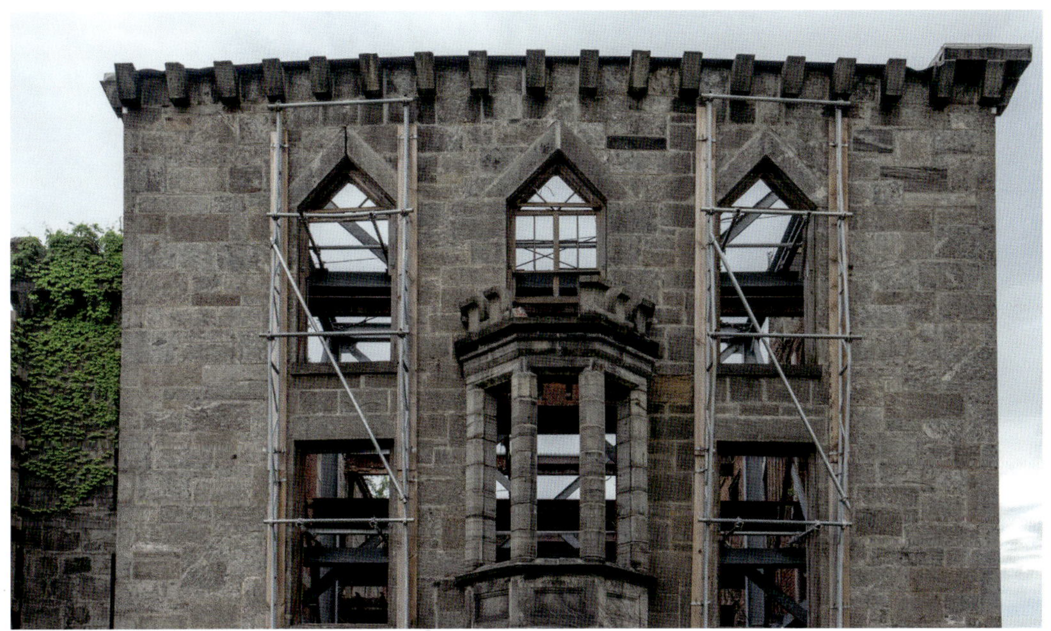

All that remains of the hospital are walls and windows. The site has been declared a New York City Landmark and is the only ruin with that designation.

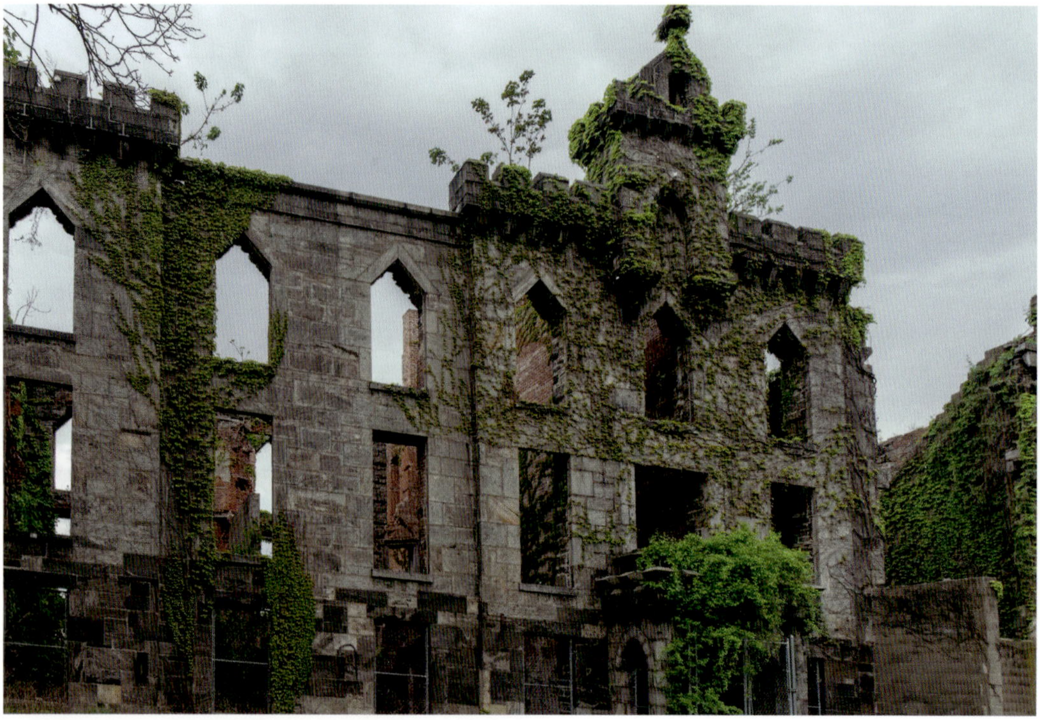

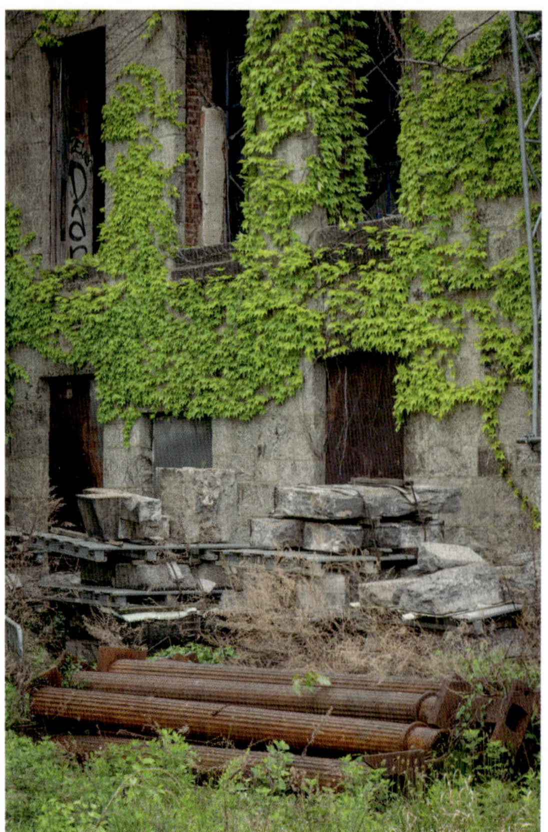

Above: Over another oriel window is a freestanding pointed arch. Plants grow inside and out, covering the facade with vines.

Left: The building is now supported by scaffolding to prevent further collapse.

9

FORT TILDEN

On the south shore of Queens lies a small spit of land that was ravaged by Hurricane Sandy in 2012. Surrounded on the north by Jamaica Bay and on the south, the Atlantic Ocean, this place is known as The Rockaways, and is also home to Fort Tilden, a serene yet dystopian-looking installation and a former U.S. Army base. A bunker sits half-buried by a sand dune. The beach is oddly abandoned, but not easy to reach either.

The Fort dates to 1917 as a defense battery to defend New York Harbor during WW II and later, WWII. During the Cold War, Fort Tilden was home to the nuclear Nike Ajax, and later, the newer Hercules missiles. The U.S. Park Service, the current custodian of the land, does little to keep the buildings from falling further into disrepair. There are only a few graffiti-laden buildings remaining on the 302 acres, and most lie behind chain-link fences and deep vegetation. The nearly empty beaches, however, are definitely worth visiting for those who enjoy solitude.

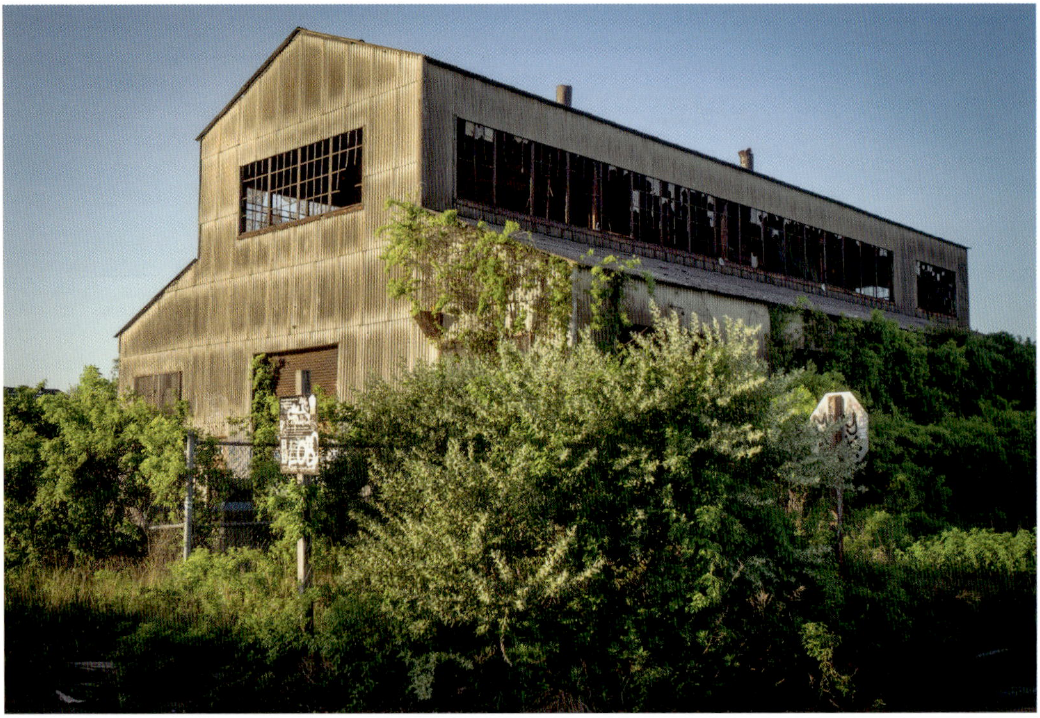

These sheds, located between the batteries at Fort Tilden, were used for ammunition storage.

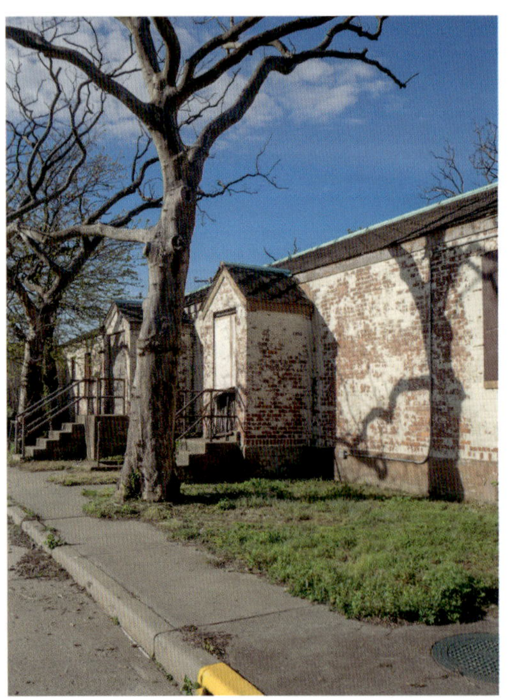

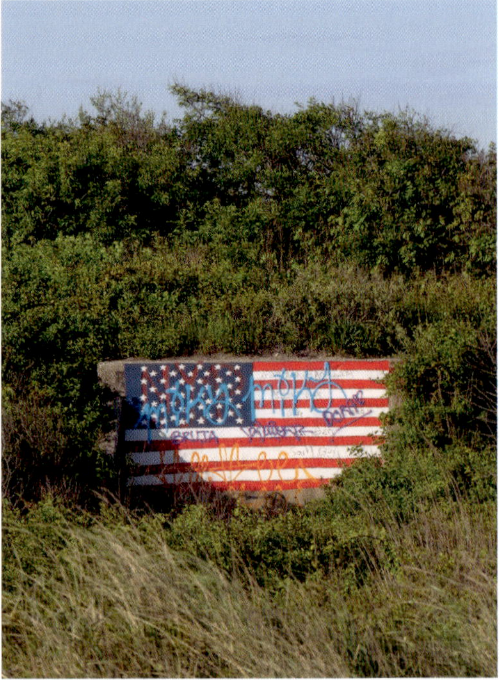

Left: These buildings appear to be housing or barracks, perhaps for the officers at the base.

Right: An American flag marks the entrance to Battery 220 at Fort Tilden, which was never completed.

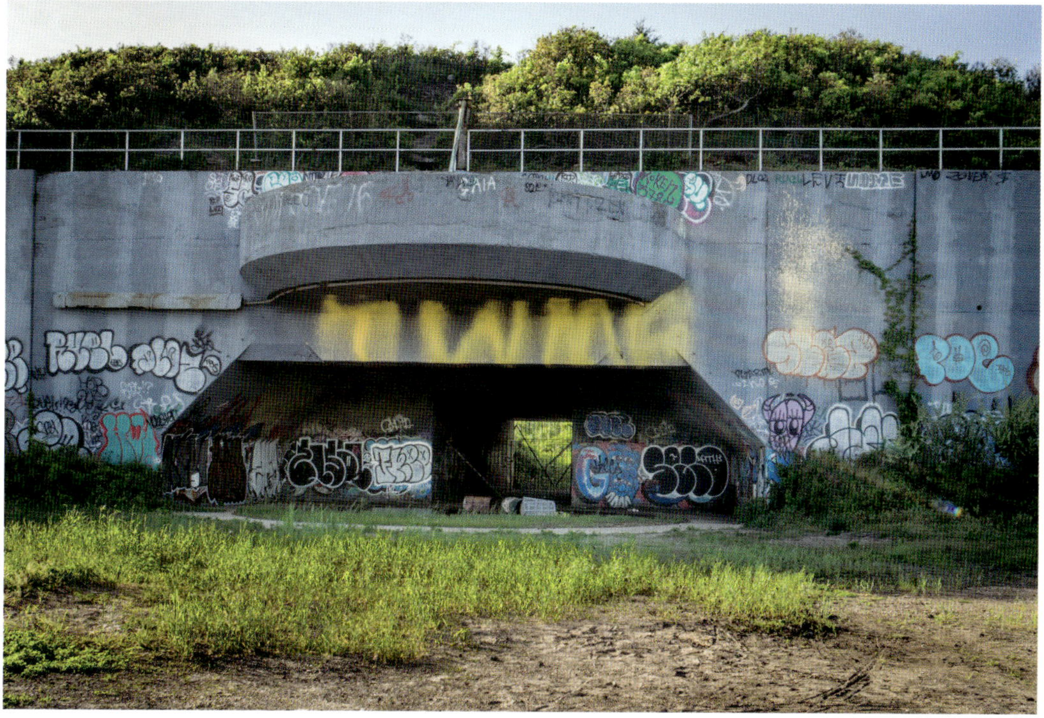

Harris Battery East was one of four batteries at Fort Tilden that protected New York from possible attacks during both World Wars. The cannons housed here were large enough to fire munitions 30 miles away.

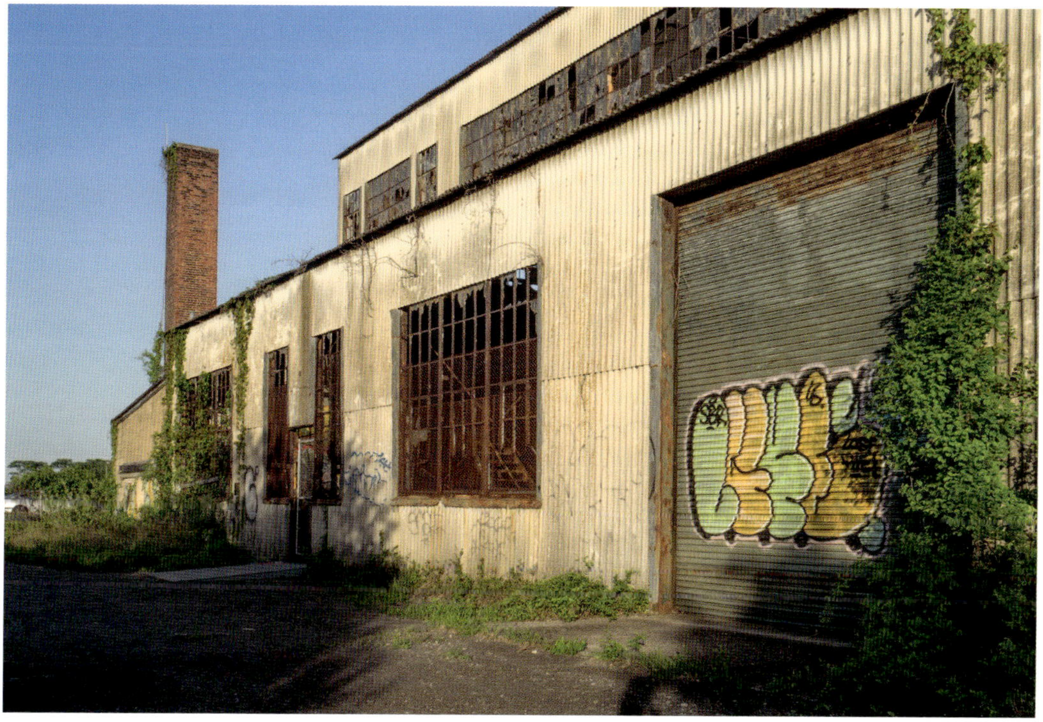

One of a few leftover buildings at the Former Army base, Fort Tilden.

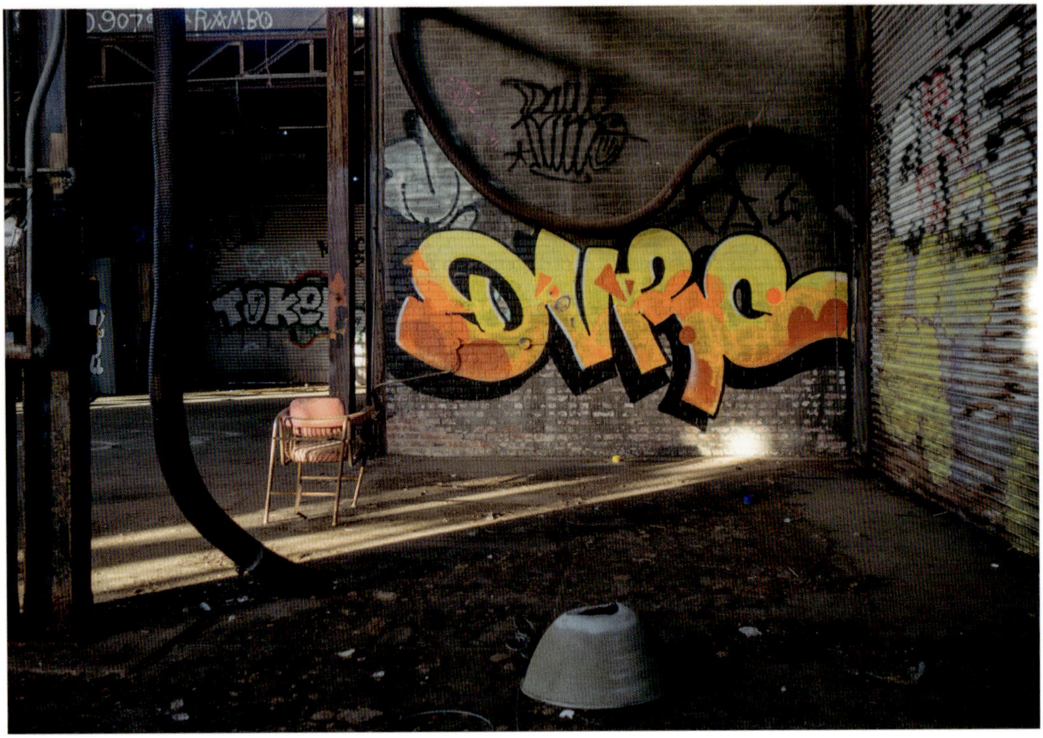

A former ammunition storage shed now houses graffiti.

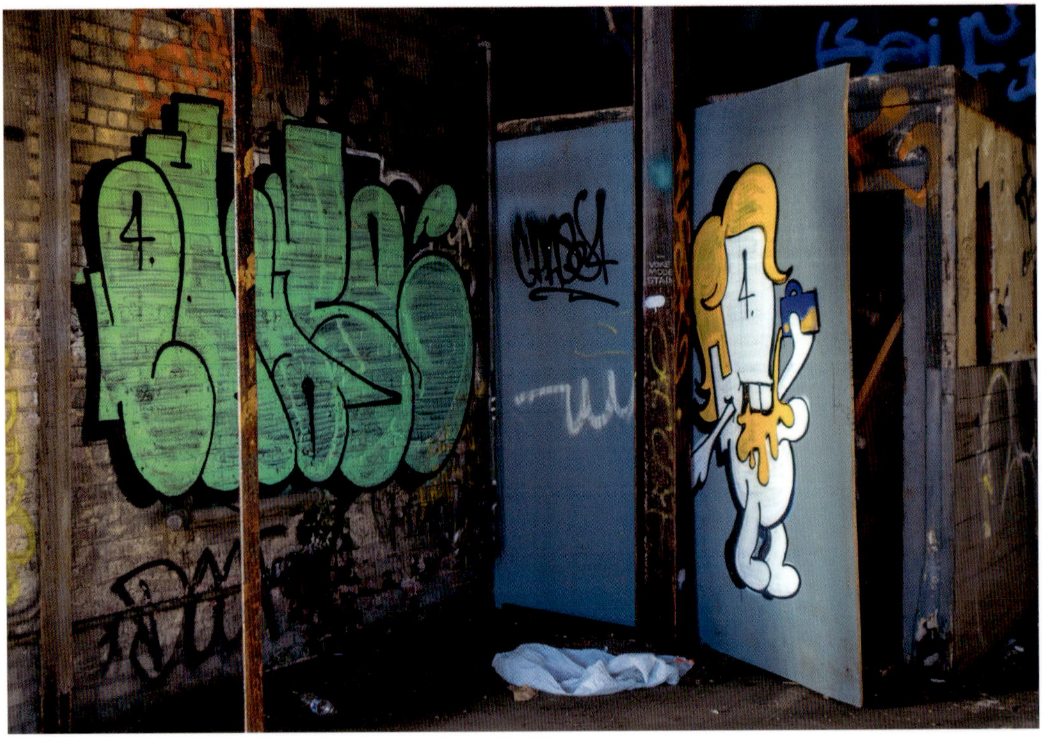

It is difficult to find a space inside this building that is not marked up with graffiti.

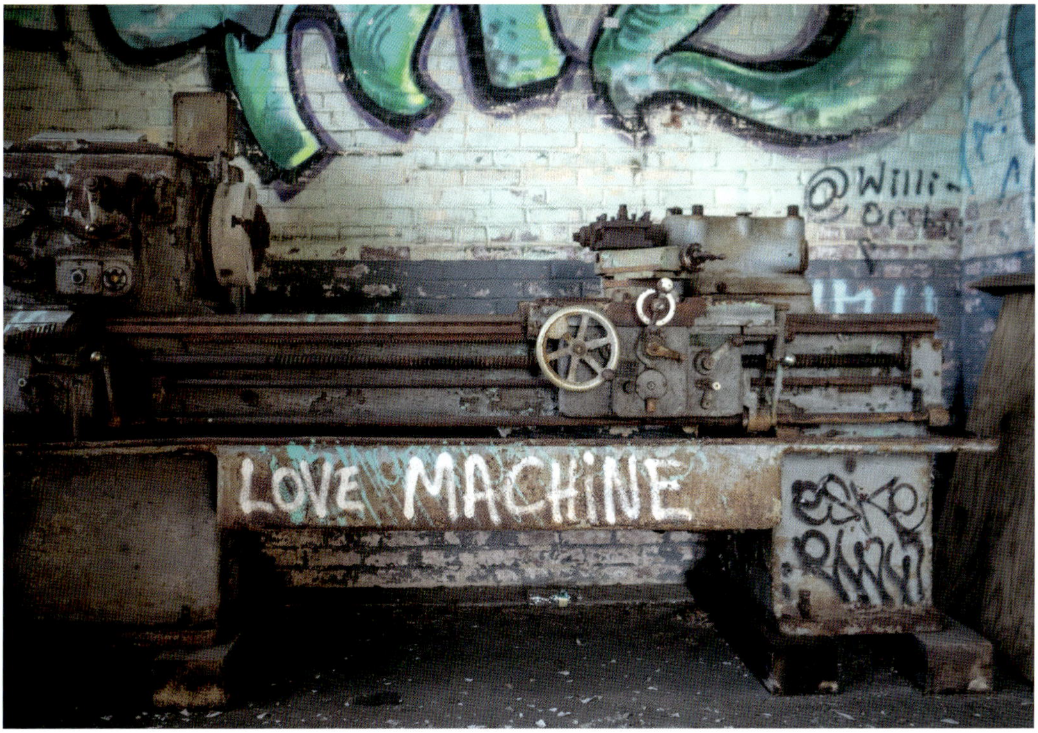

A lone machine inside the ammunition storage shed.

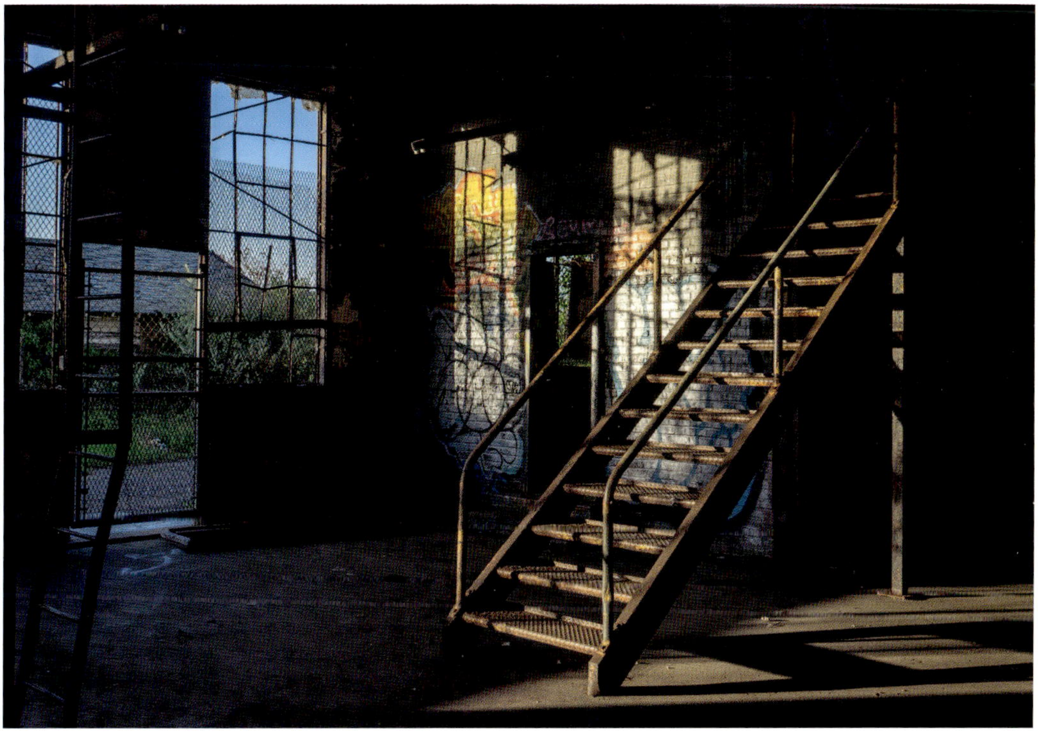

More graffiti …

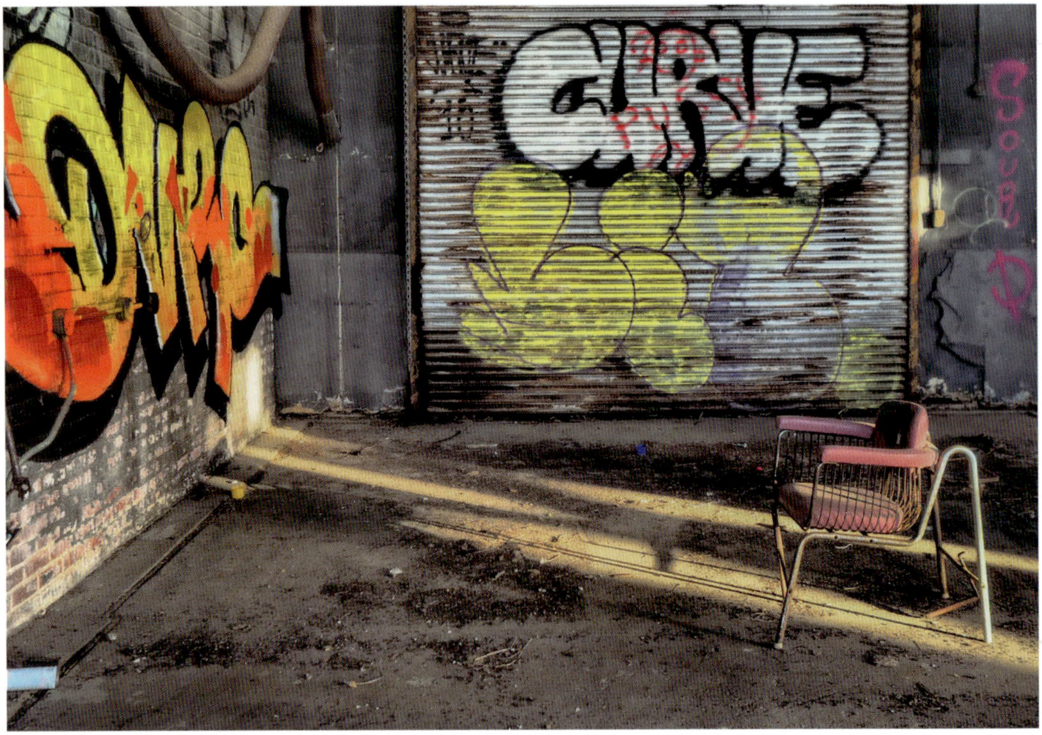

… and still more.

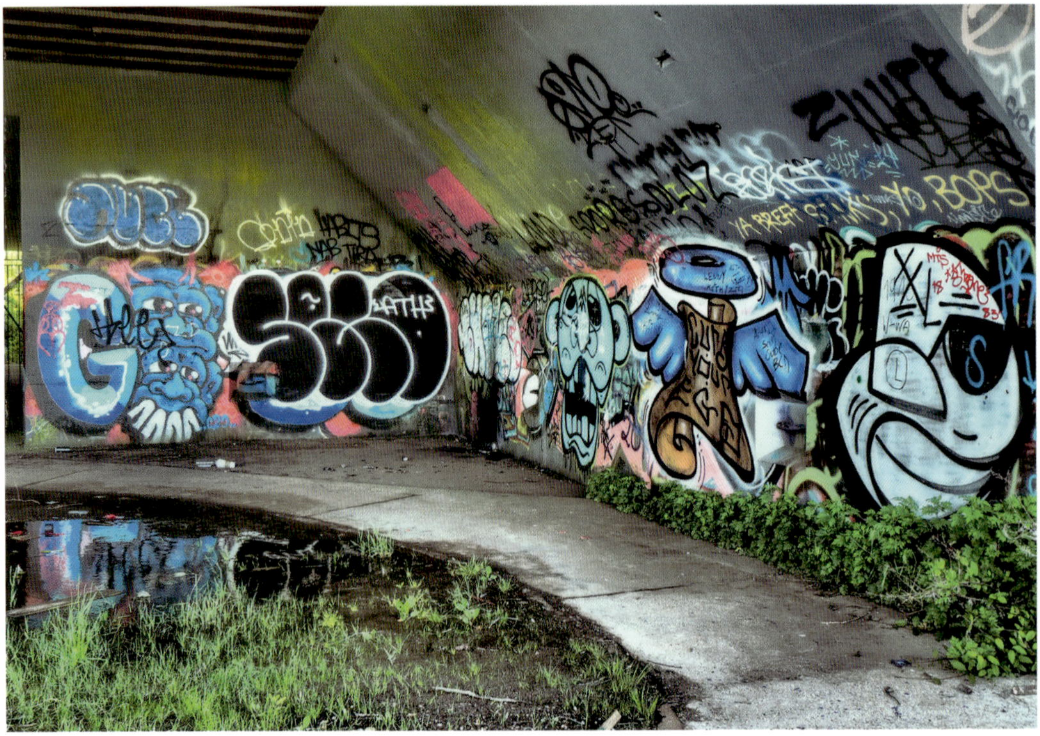

The interior of Harris Battery East is now filled with graffiti instead of cannons and mortar shells.

10

FLOYD BENNETT FIELD

Floyd Bennett Field, another abandoned piece of U.S. history, sits across the bay from Fort Tilden. Bennett Field played an essential role in America's past, especially in the capacity of aviation. The airfield, named after Floyd Bennett, a Navy flyer who piloted the flight over the North Pole with Commander Richard E. Byrd in 1926, opened as New York City's first municipal airport on May 23, 1931.

The airfield consists of four concrete runways, four hangars, and a large administration/terminal building. Once constructed, this was the most modern airport in the world. Hotshot would-be record breakers loved the airport for its long, concrete runways and its proximity to the east coast for transatlantic flights. For example, Wiley Post made the first solo around-the-world trip, covering 15,957 miles in seven days, eighteen hours, forty-five minutes, and five seconds. A vast crowd was there to greet him on his return at Bennett Field on July 15, 1933. Five years later, Howard Hughes beat that record by nearly three full days.

A mere ten years after the airfield's opening, LaGuardia Airport (then called Municipal Airfield #2) opened and soon, the money-strapped Bennett Field was sold to the Navy and became the busiest military airfield in the country during WWII. Floyd Bennett Field was decommissioned in 1971 and soon after became part of the National Park Service.

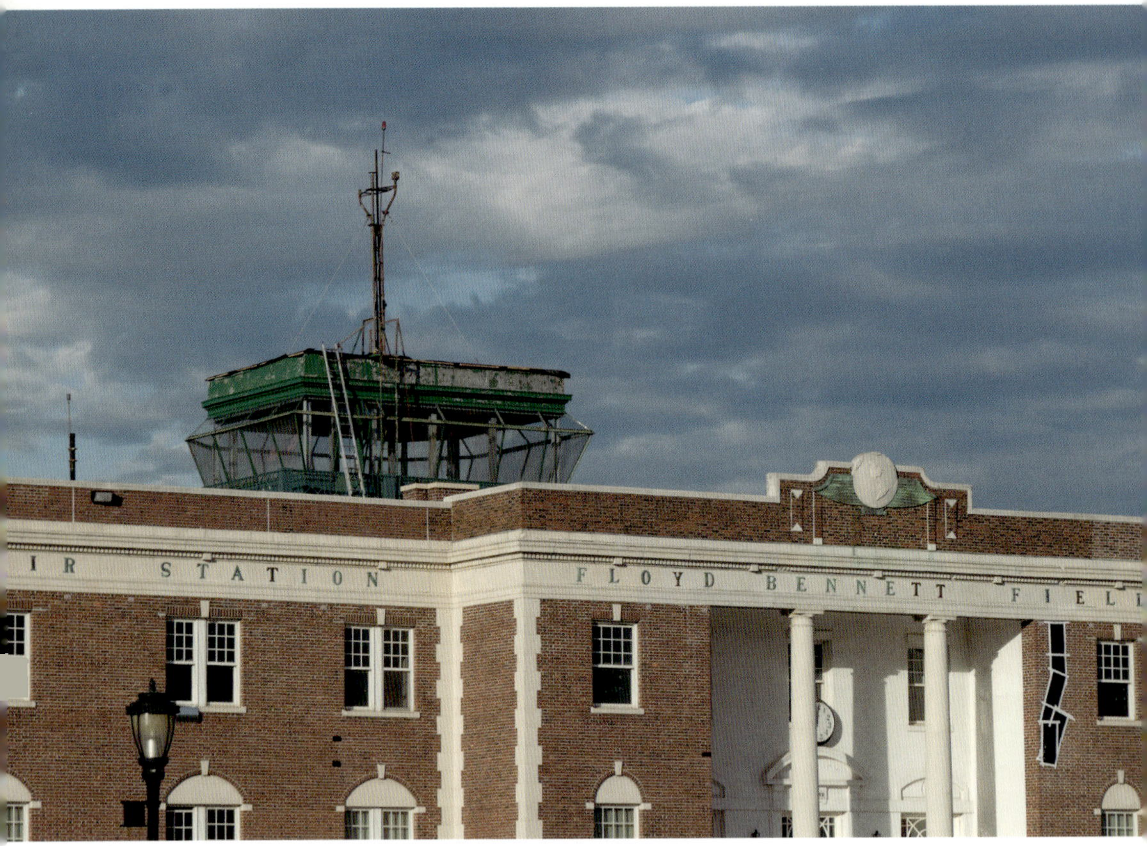

Floyd Bennett Field lies at the very end of Flatbush Ave., on Barren Island in the Jamaica Bay.

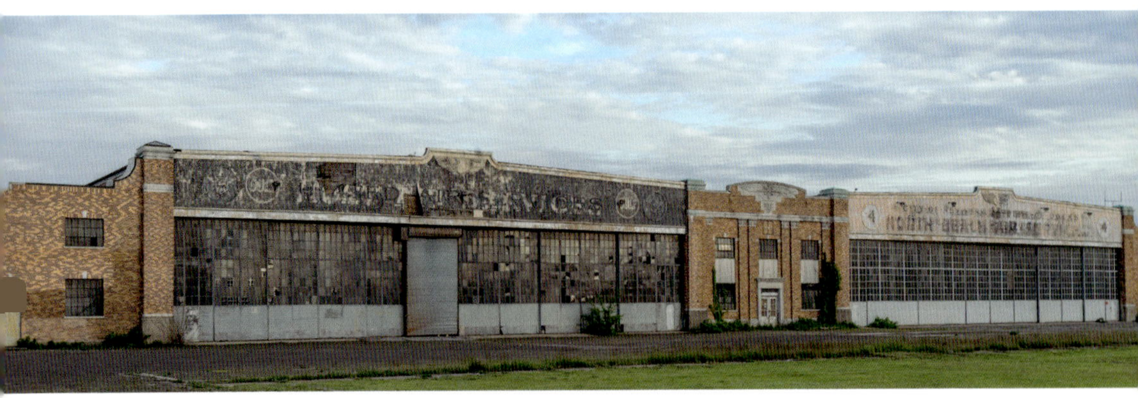

Two of the four old hangars at Floyd Bennett Field.

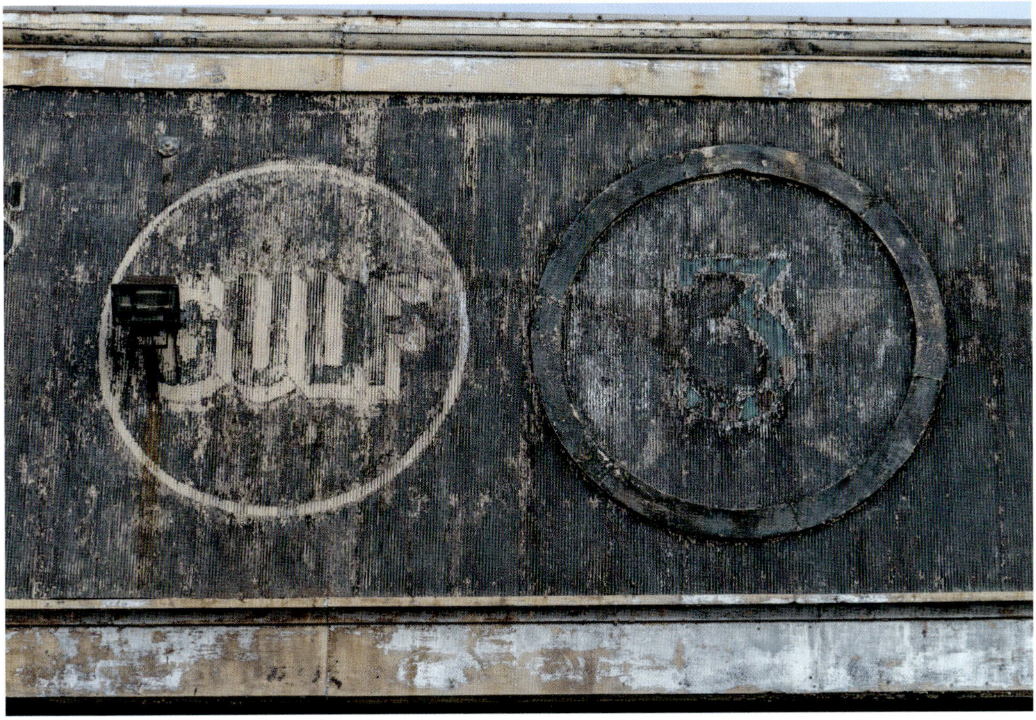

Above: A detail of the top of the hangar shows that this was hangar #3 and had Gulf fuel available.

Right: This hanger door has some very nice Art Deco features.

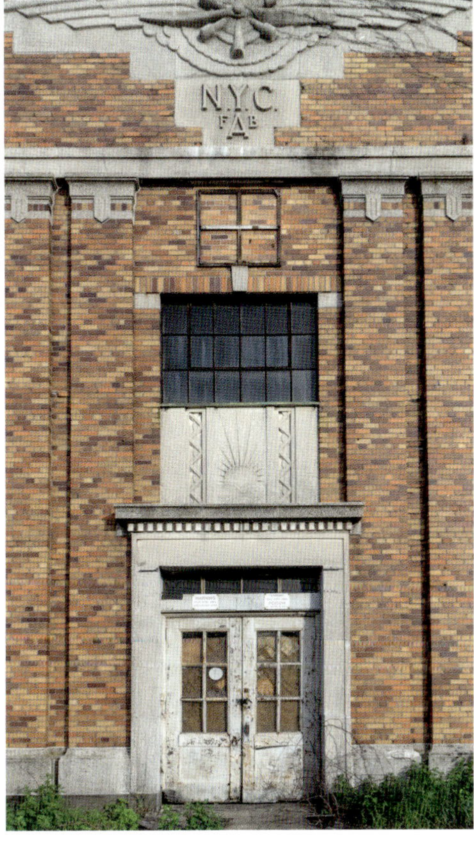

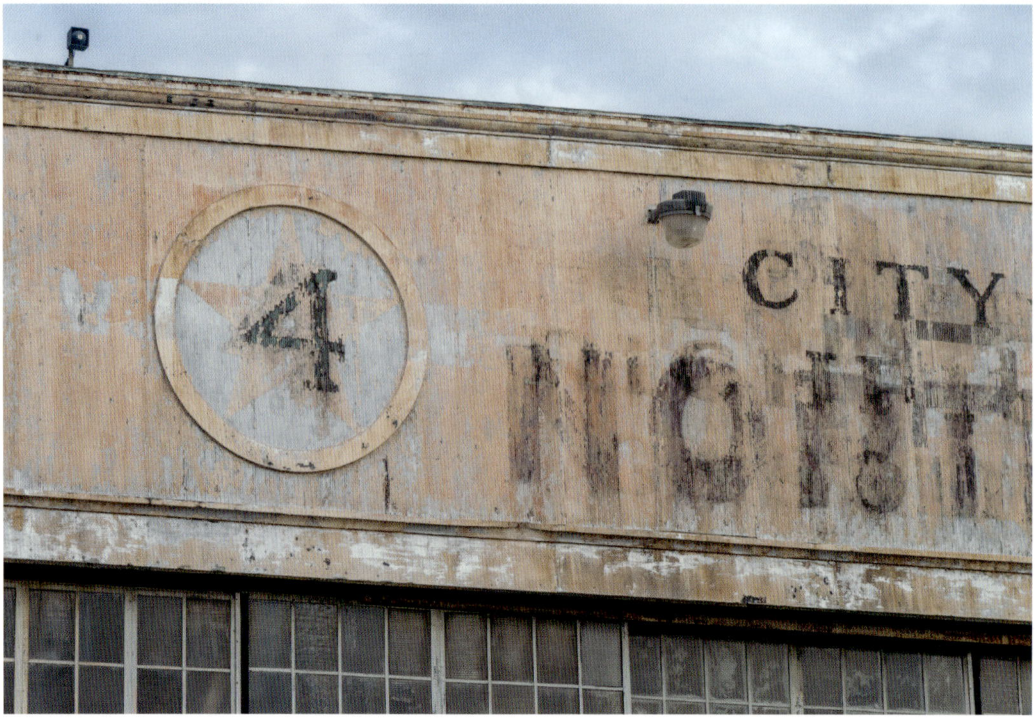

Hangar #4.

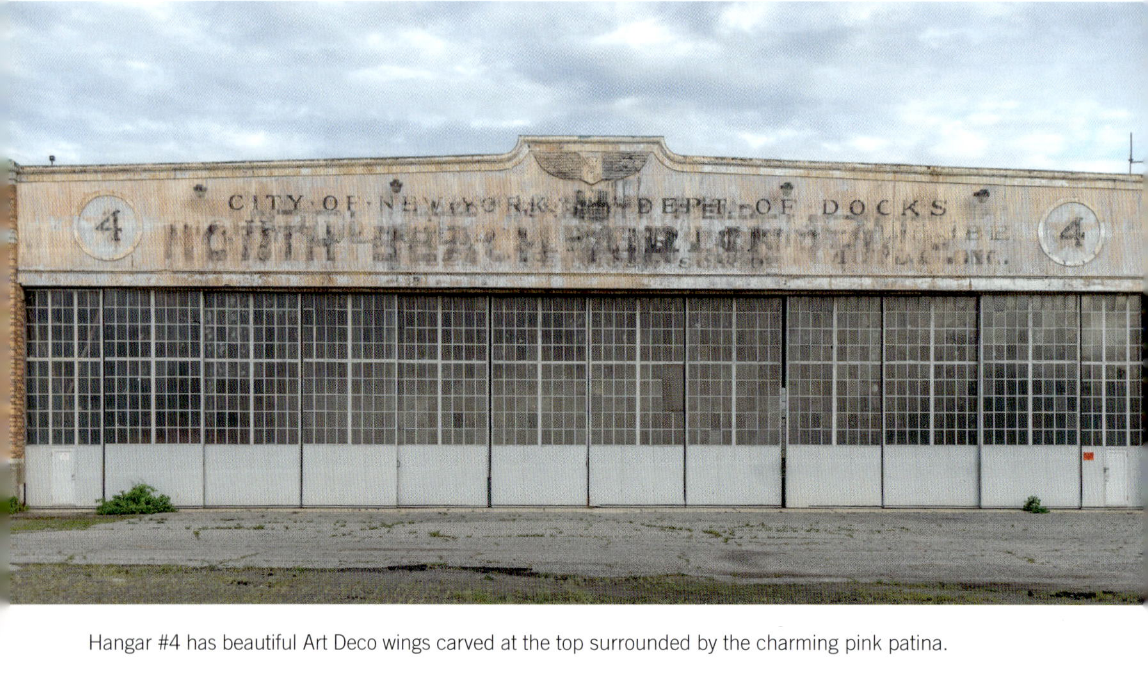

Hangar #4 has beautiful Art Deco wings carved at the top surrounded by the charming pink patina.

11

CORONA PARK

Tucked away in Queens near what is now called Arthur Ashe Stadium and Citifield, where the Mets play, one finds the remarkable remnants of the 1939 and 1964 New York World's Fair. The site, a former swamp and ash dump, was filled in and converted into a 1,200-acre park in the late 1930s. The park was conceived by Robert Moses, New York's park commissioner, a polarizing urban developer, and famous for favoring highways over public transportation. This park is miles away from the urban center of Manhattan.

As I grew up on Long Island, we would see the gargantuan Unisphere globe each time we drove by it on the Long Island Expressway. The theme of the 1964 World's Fair focused on the future and the Space Age. The Unisphere was designed to embrace this concept. Corona Park is also home to the Queens Science Museum, a surviving leftover building form the 1939 World's Fair. This building was also used at the 1964 fair to display a panorama of New York built by Robert Moses. This panorama features every building in New York at the time, and is still housed here in a special exhibit room.

The fair site also contains the New York State Pavilion, which was declared a historic landmark only a few years ago. Now, with an infusion of new funding, the structure is being restored. Three tall futuristic-looking observation decks of different heights flanked the building pavilion. The top was reached by a "Sky Streak capsule" elevator for a fee. The lowest tower was a VIP deck. The building itself is elliptical and the inside was painted a color called "American Cheese Yellow." On the floor was a fascinating feature, a giant inlay terrazzo map of New York, sponsored by Texaco and thus called the Texaco Map. Every Texaco station in the state was accurately placed on the map. Parts of it still remain after years of weather and abuse; volunteers are painstakingly restoring it piece by piece.

The 1964 World's Fair was a nod to technology and the Space Age, so there were numerous exhibits featuring these themes. The New York Pavilion was aptly named the "Tent of Tomorrow."

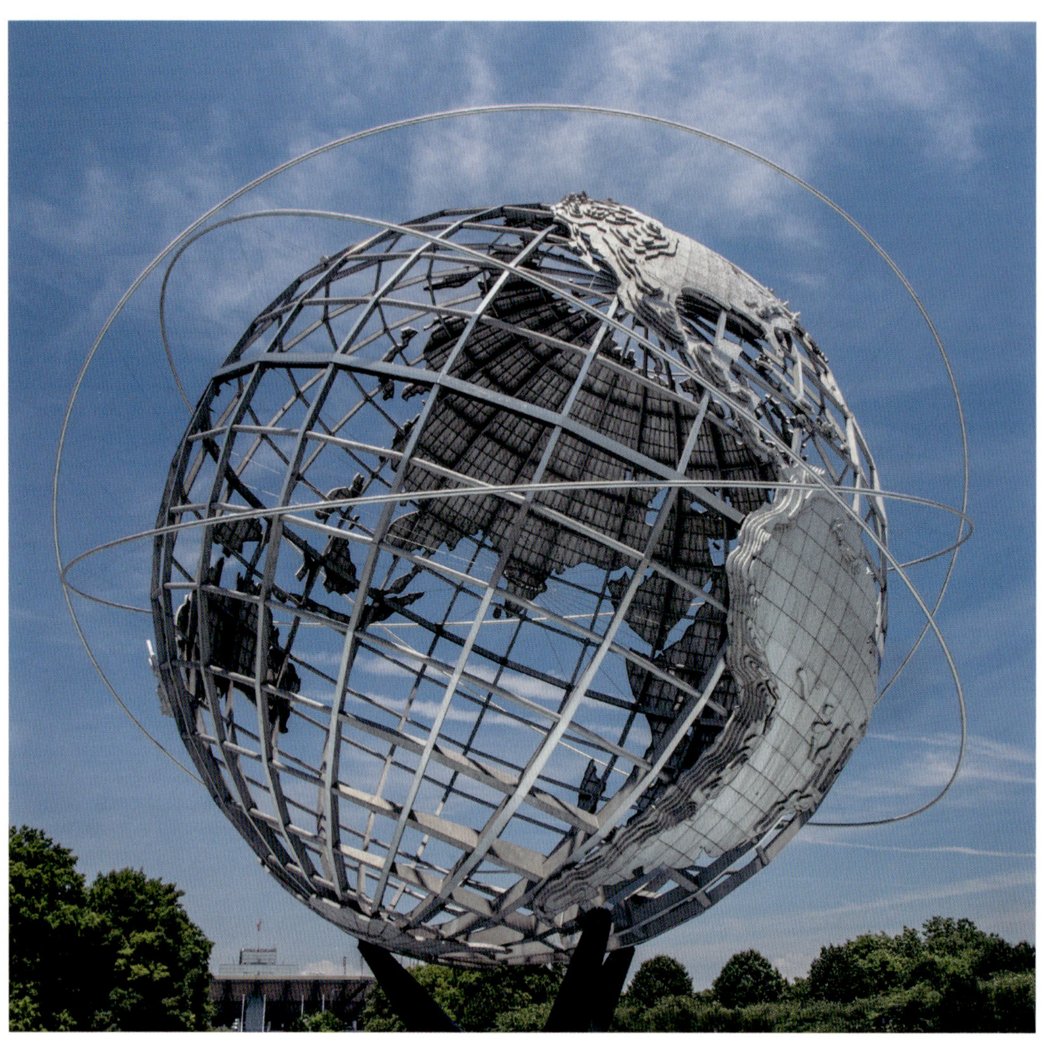

The iconic Unisphere at the 1964 World's Fair site in Queens.

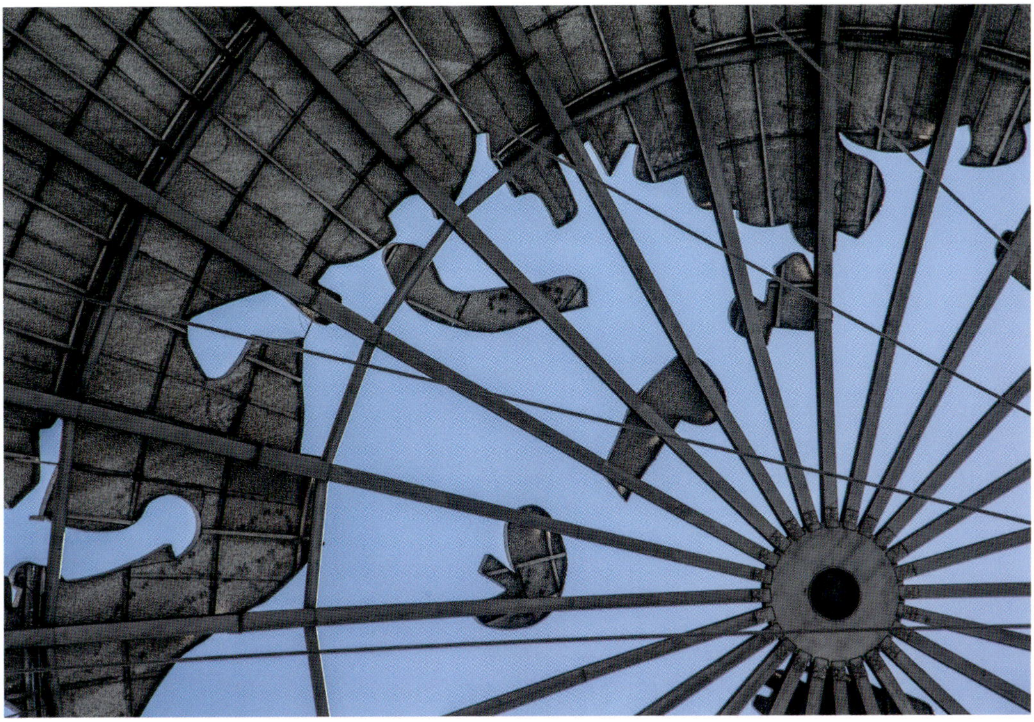

Above: Looking up inside the Unisphere. The Unisphere rises 140 in the air, with a diameter of 120 feet.

Right: The other two observation towers flank the side of the pavilion.

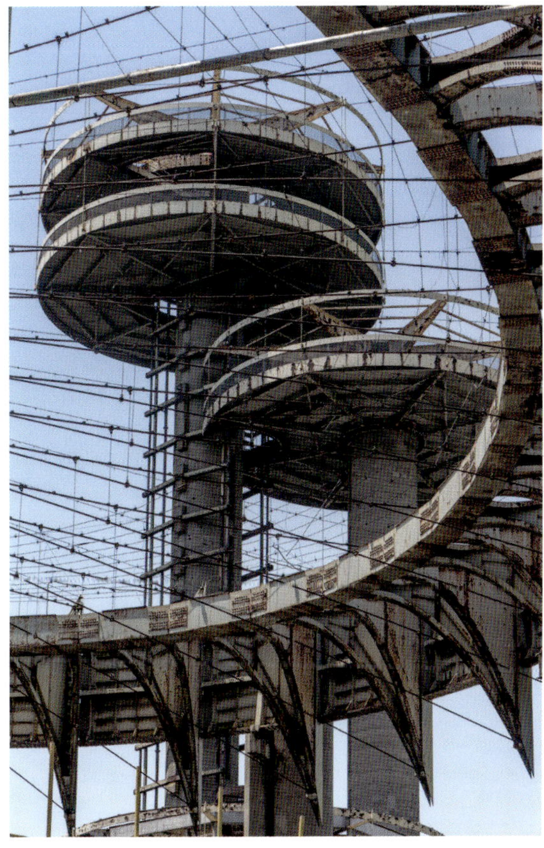

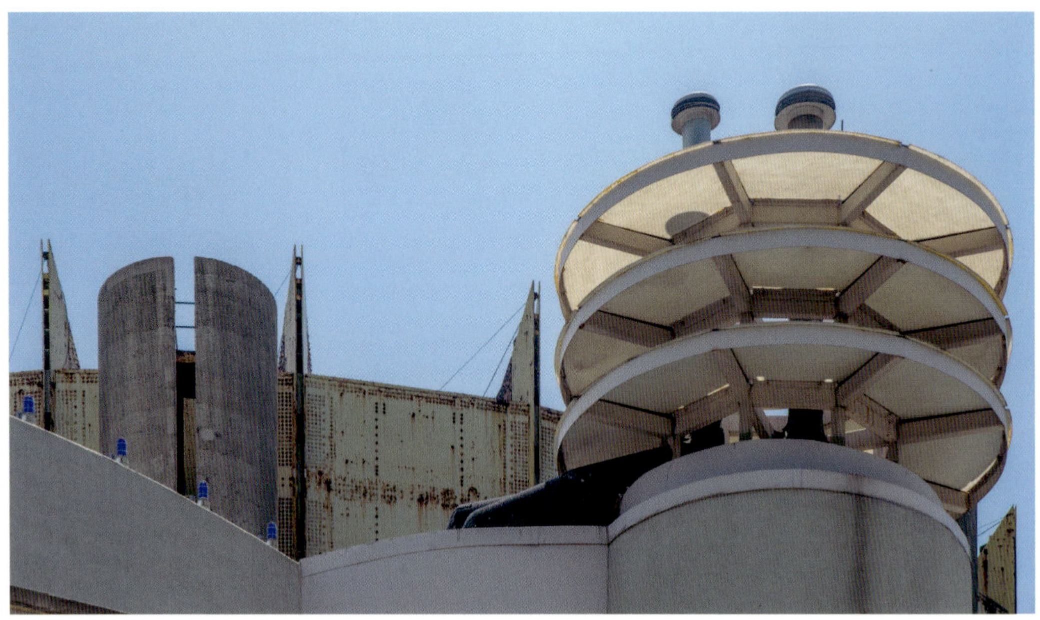

Two of these circular caps adorned the outside of the building that was known as Theatrerama. Today it is used as a live stage, called Queen's Theater.

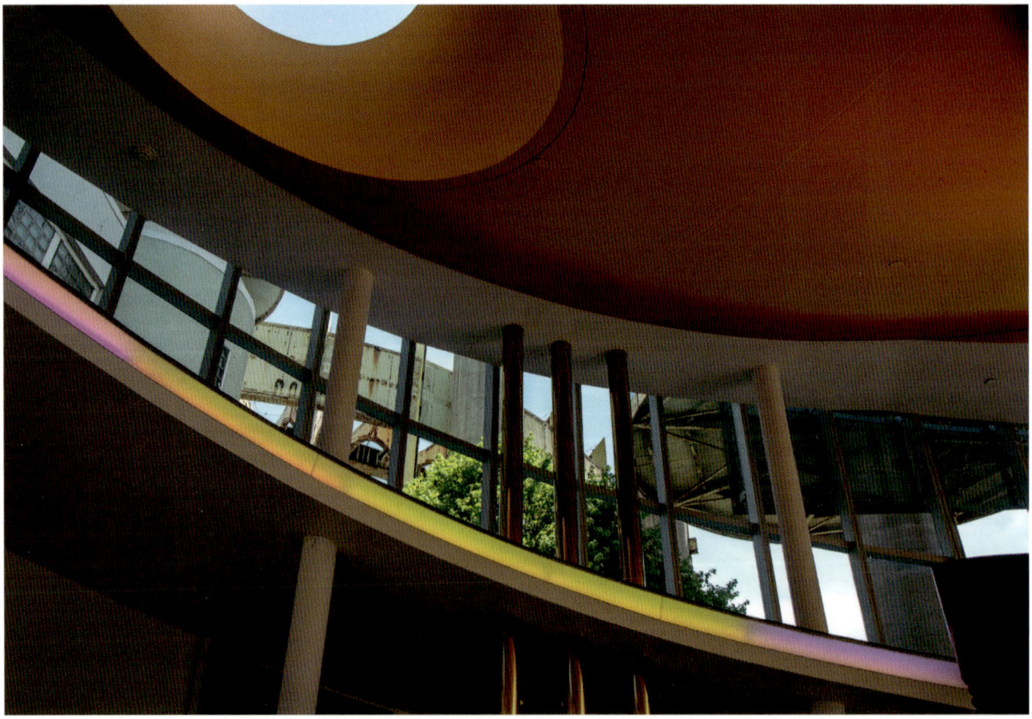

Queen's Theater is a transparent circular theater offering views of the New York Pavilion. Portions can be used as a party room for residents of the borough of Queens, according to the restoration designers Caples Jefferson Architects.

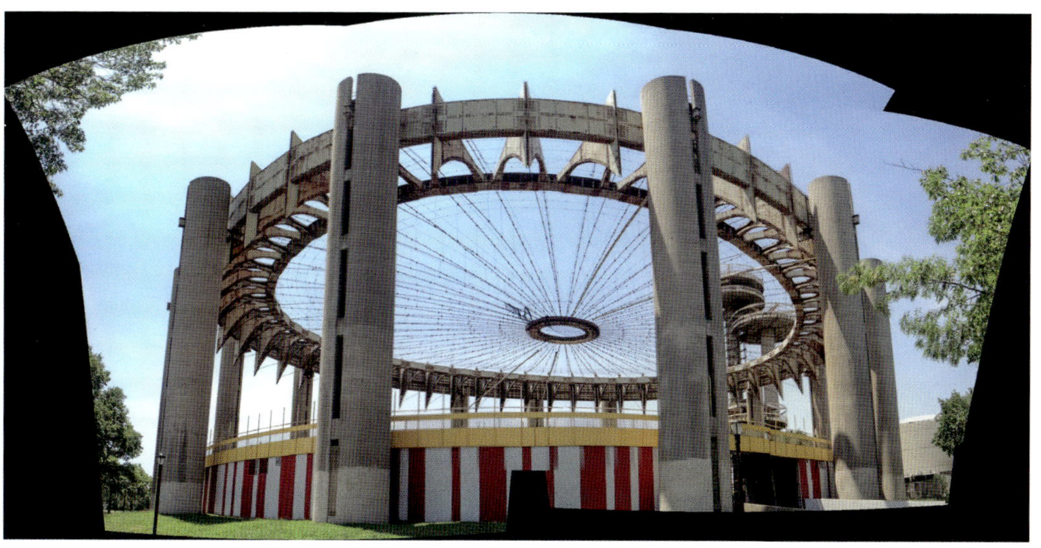

The futuristic looking New York Pavilion at Corona Park in Queens.

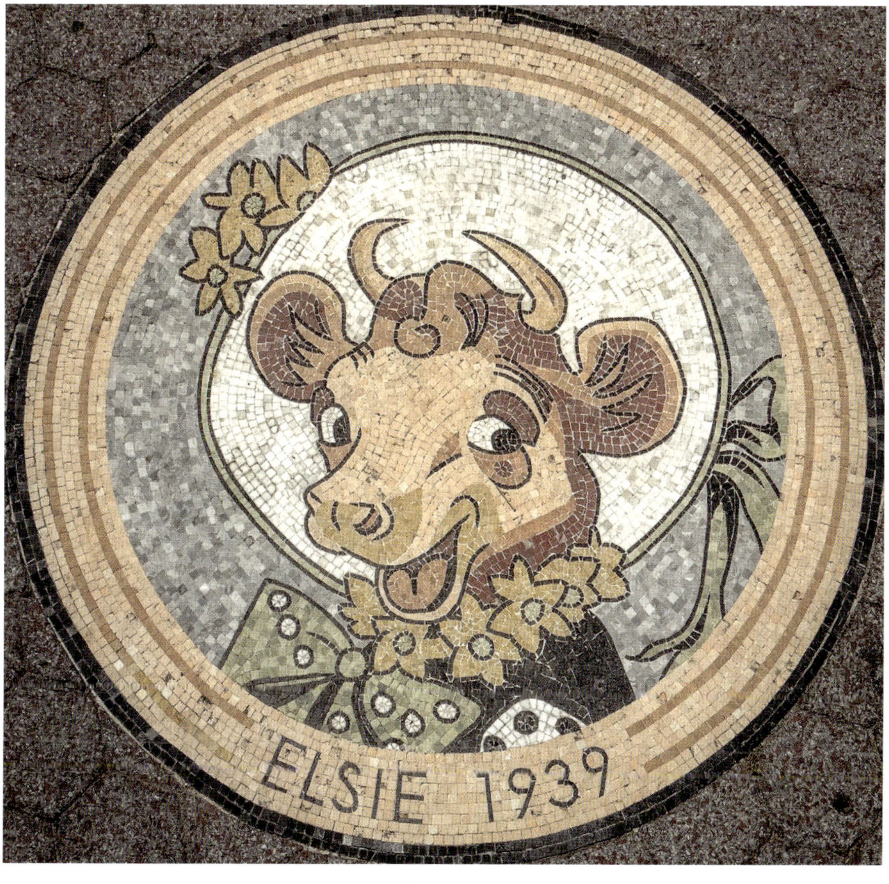

Elsie, Borden Dairy Company's bovine mascot, is a mosaic enshrined in the sidewalk at the 1939 World's Fair site. Elsie was a real cow on display at the fair.

12

ODDS AND ENDS

There are so many nooks and crannies in the City of New York that it would be an impossible task to document all of them. I tried to include some of the more curious places in this section I have discovered over the years. Not all these oddities are abandoned, and some are no longer available to see. From flea markets and tiny statues to faded ads to a Trash Museum, the City of Dreams has something for everyone.

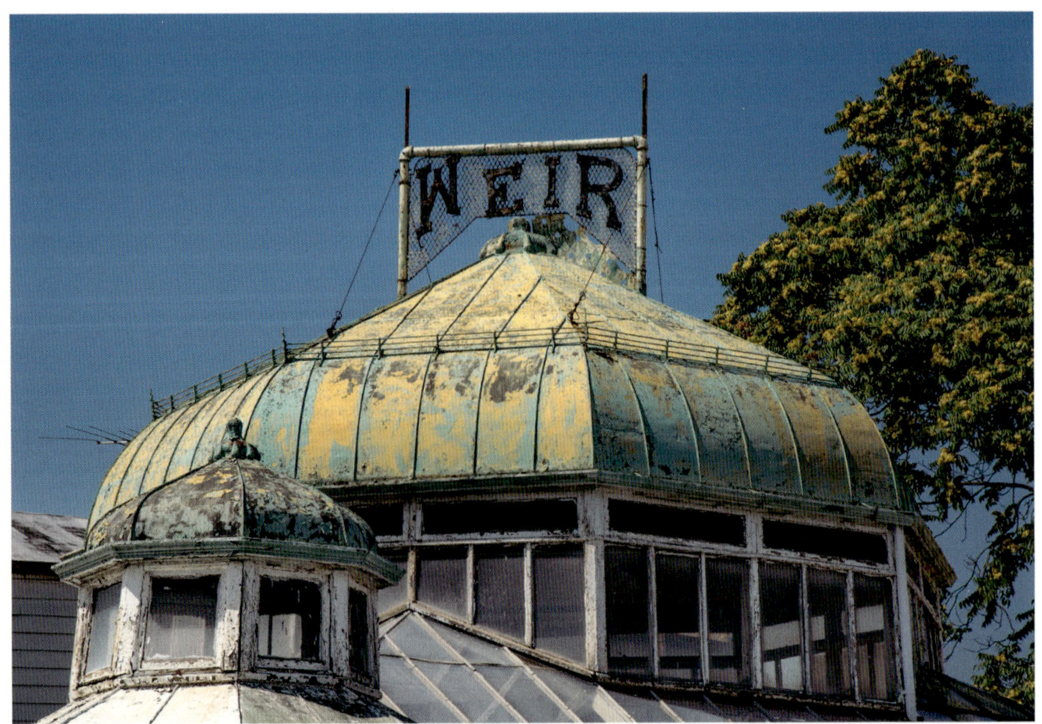

The Weir greenhouse with its iconic copper roof dates from the 1850s and is currently being restored. It is one of two surviving Victorian-style greenhouses in the City of New York.

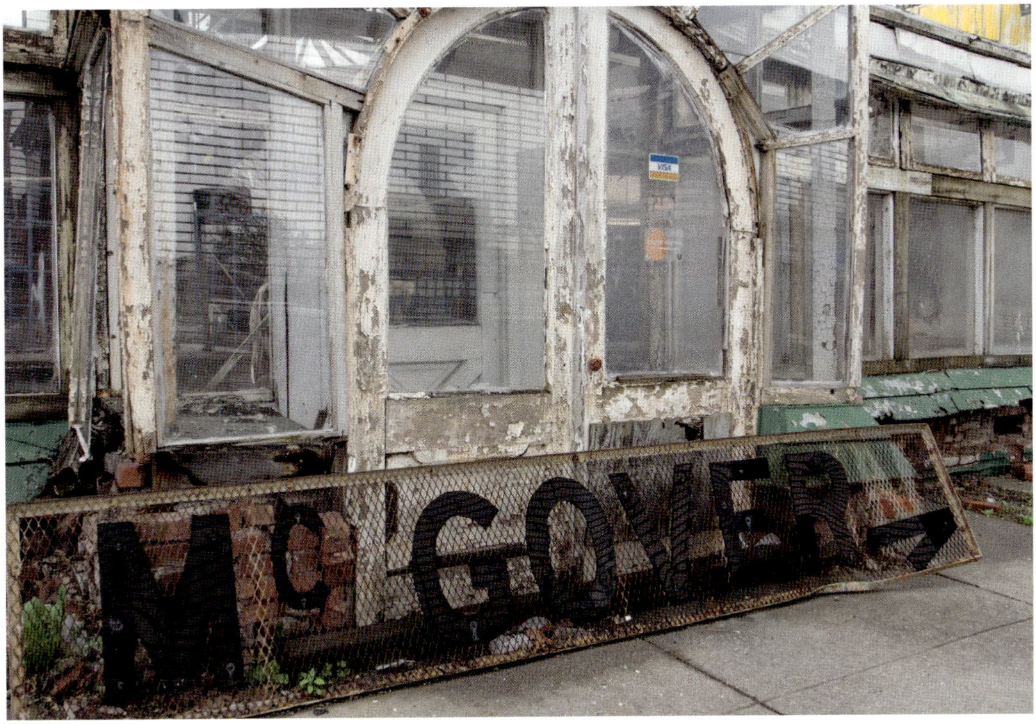

The rare McGovern Weir building will be part of a visitors' center for Green-Wood Cemetery across the street. For more than seventy-five years, from 1895 until 1971, Weir greenhouse served the grieving people of Brooklyn who were visiting the cemetery.

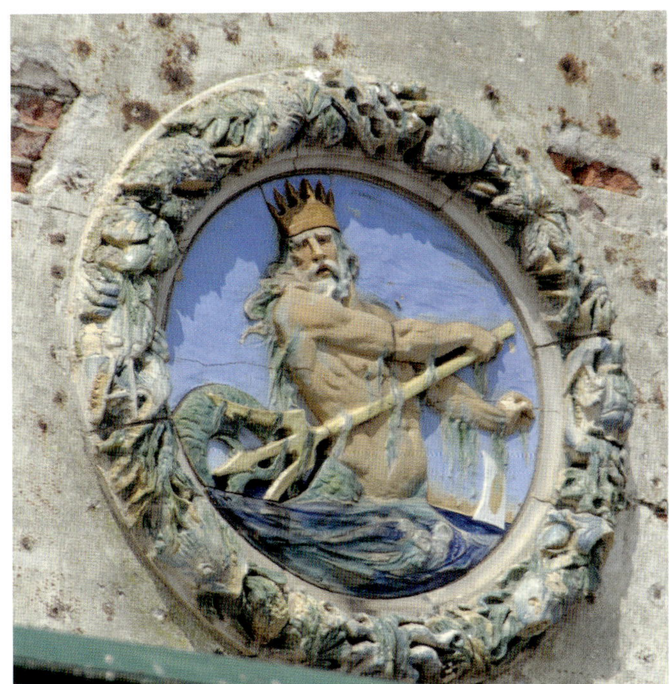

Detail of an abandoned building in Coney Island built in 1923 that was once Childs Restaurant. The side of the building is bedecked with these fantastic nautical-themed terra cotta emblems. The building was restored in 2017 and is now open to the public.

This iconic face, in spite of popular belief, has no name, and is simply called "Funny Face." He has been the face of Coney Island, specifically Steeplechase Park, since around 1907. George C. Tilyou, founder of the park, created the face. Steeplechase Park closed in 1964. Fred Trump bought the property in 1966 and bulldozed it all, including Funny Face. Funny Face has a cousin in Asbury Park, New Jersey, where Tilyou opened a second park. The newer face is known as Tillie.

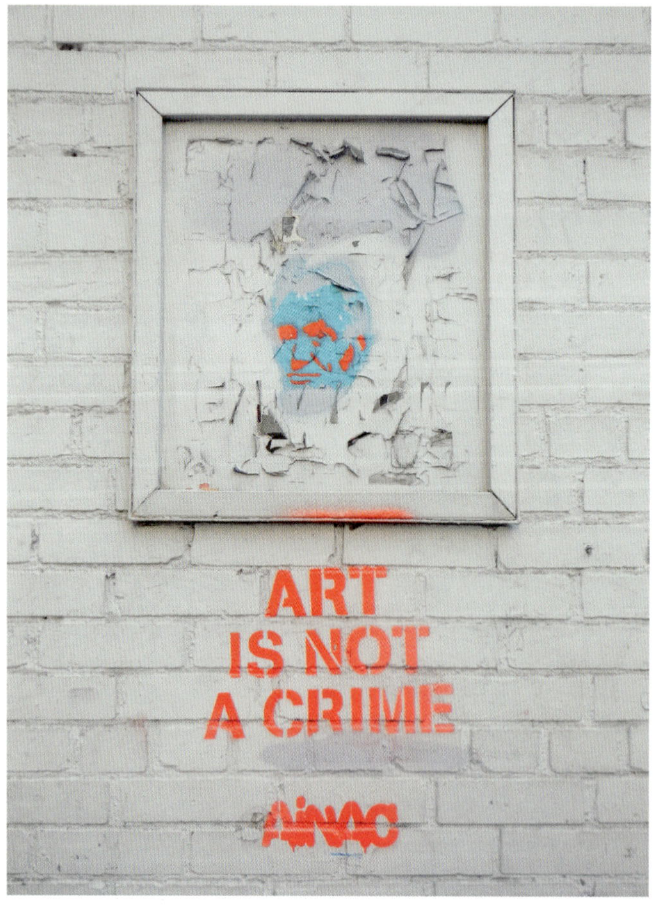

New York City has hundreds of miles of wall space, and some graffiti artists cannot seem to help themselves. But I will agree with this one: art is not a crime.

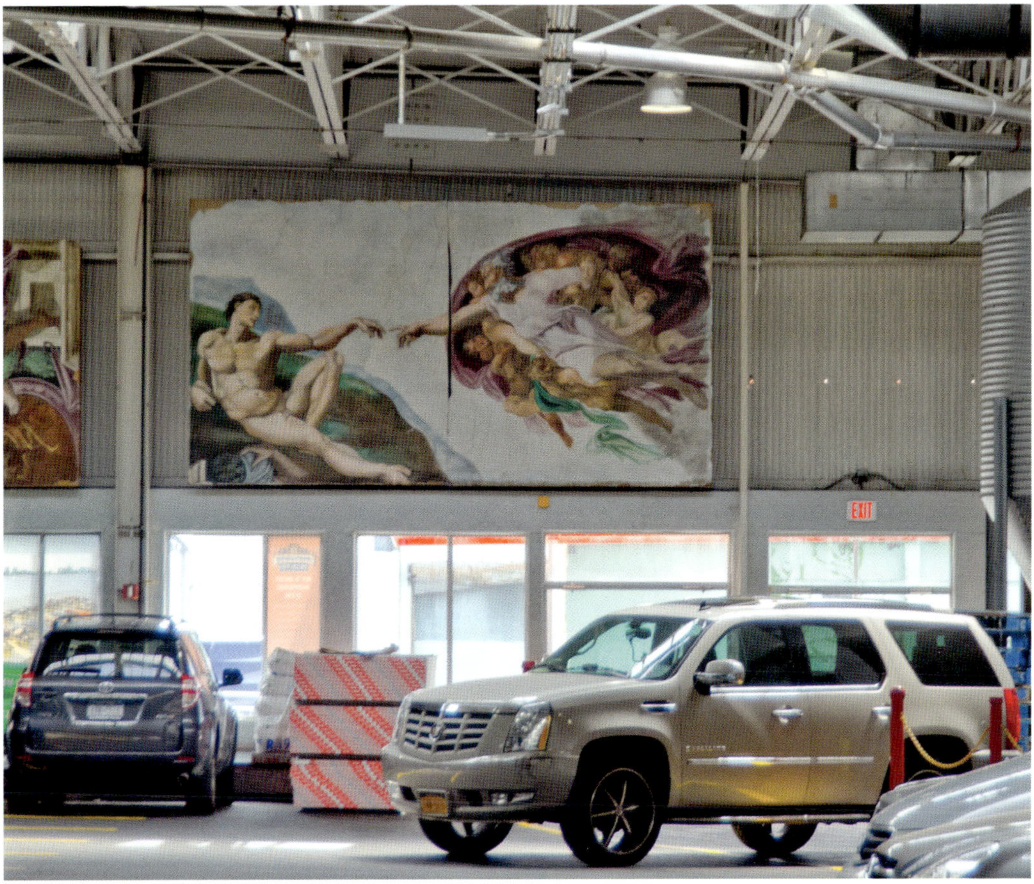

Above: This parking garage seems to have a bit of an attitude.

Right: Another piece of well-executed graffiti down by the Brooklyn Bridge caught my attention.

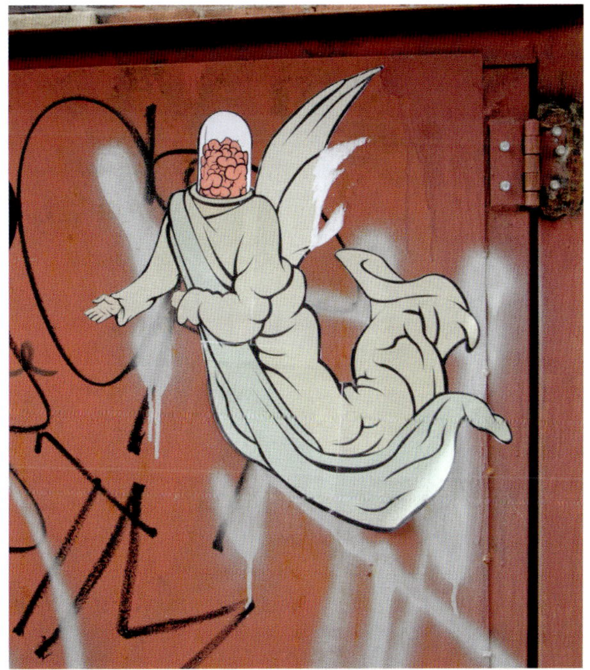

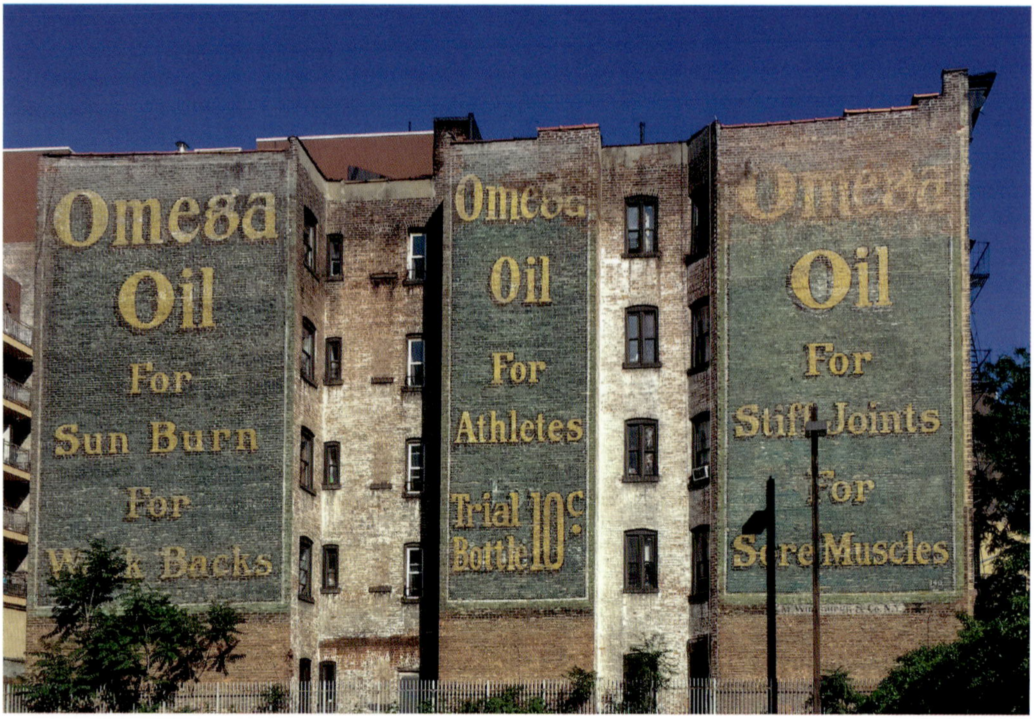

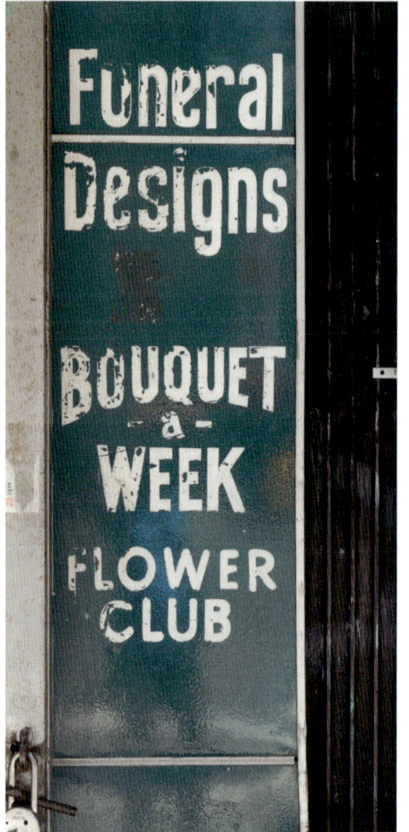

Above: Harlem is home to a particularly good example of a well-preserved ghost sign for Omega Oil. Omega Oil was an all-purpose oil that probably amounted to no more than snake oil.

Left: An ironic old sign, not quite a ghost sign, graces the side of a door.

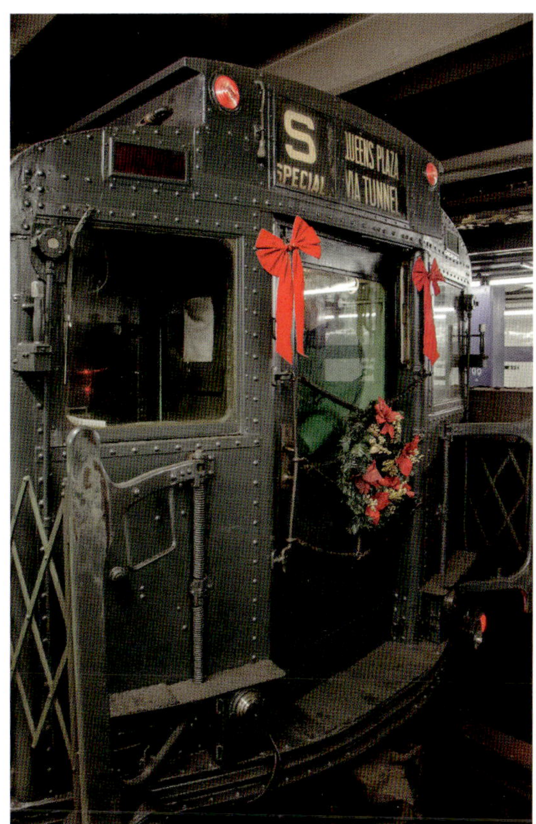

Right: The "Holiday Nostalgia Train" rides the rails of the New York subway system in the weeks preceding Christmas on the F line.

Below: The subway cars are original, each car depicting a different era.

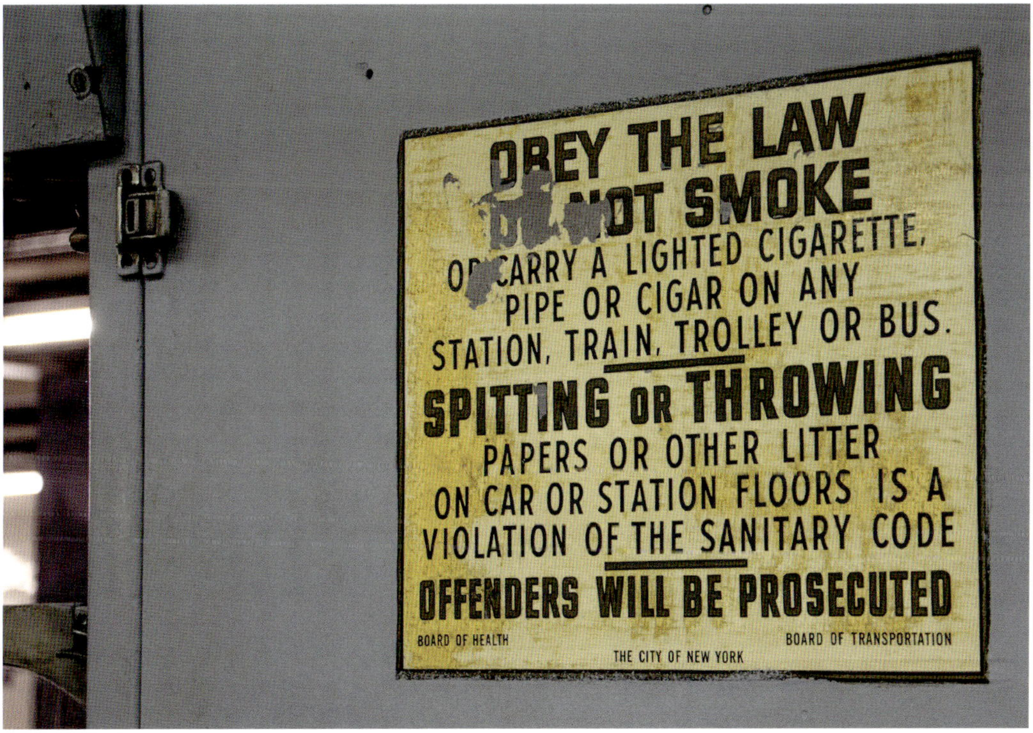

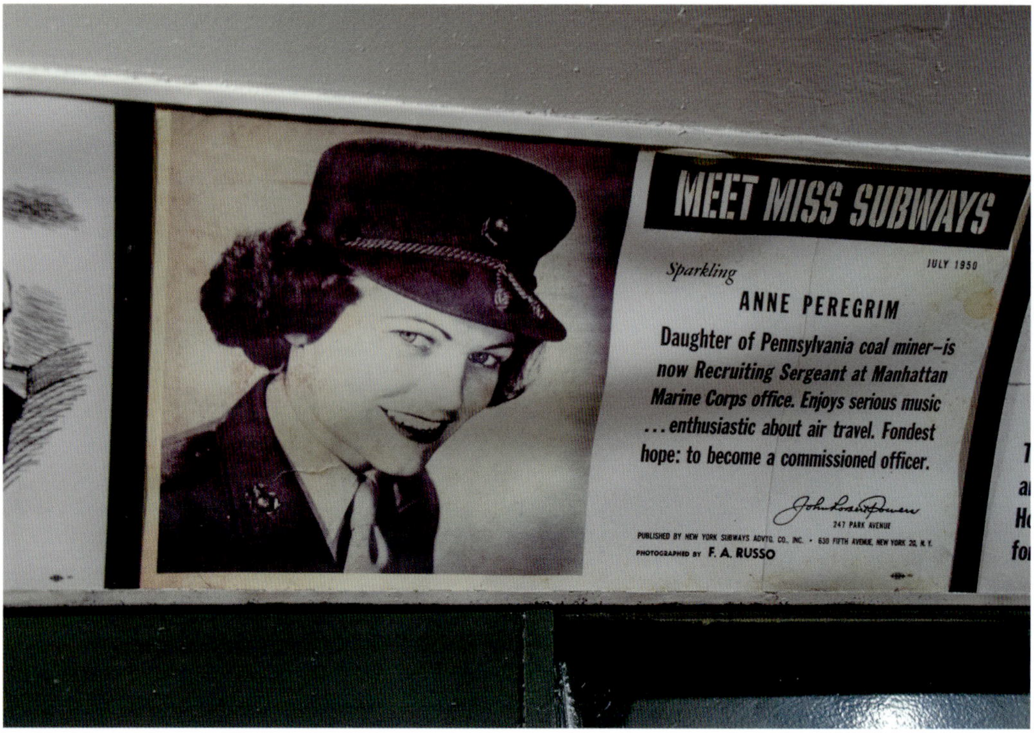

The subway cars also feature vintage ads from the period that each car represents.

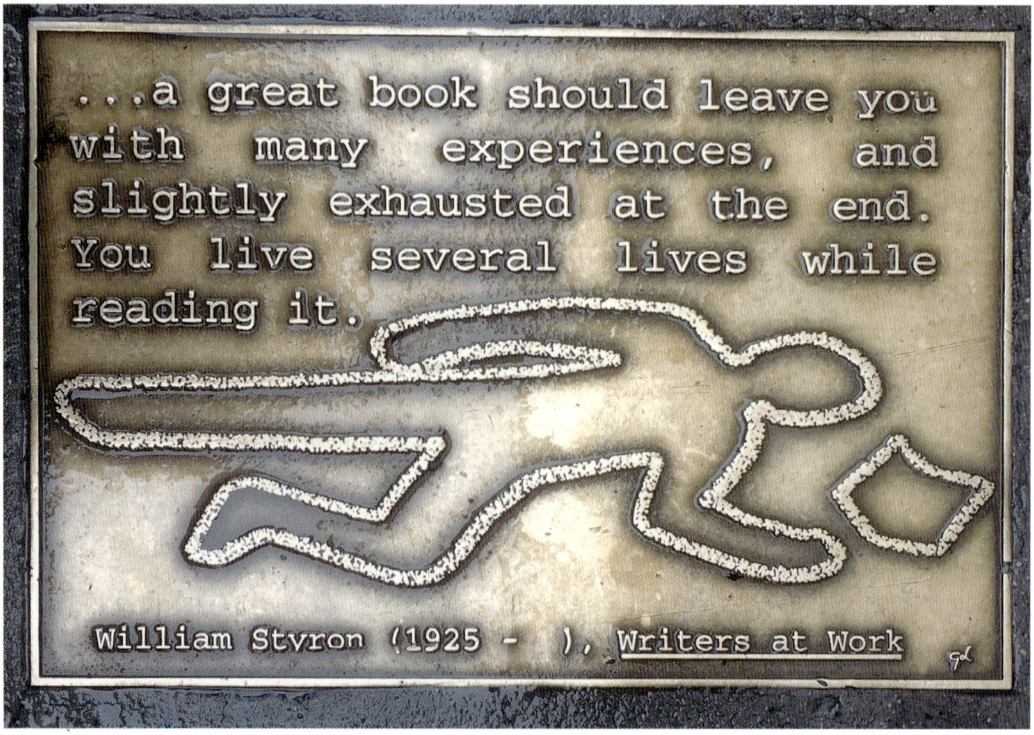

Bronze plaques such as these are embedded in the sidewalks on the streets surrounding the New York Public Library.

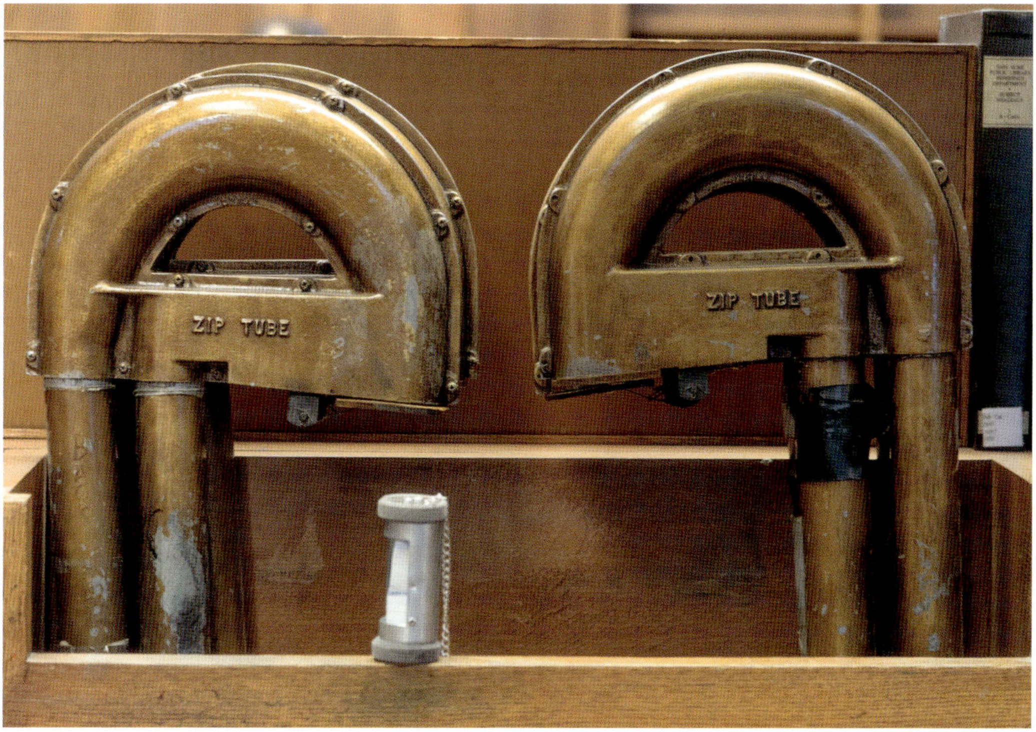

Above: Old disused pneumatic tubes at the New York Public Library were once used to transmit requests and information between its seven floors.

Right: The Marine Merchant Memorial, half in water, half out, located at Battery Park, depicts a mariner drowning while another tries to save him. A third man calls for help, and a fourth mariner is in shock on his knees. At high tide, the mariner in the water drowns, twice a day. It is based on a photograph of an actual event during WWII.

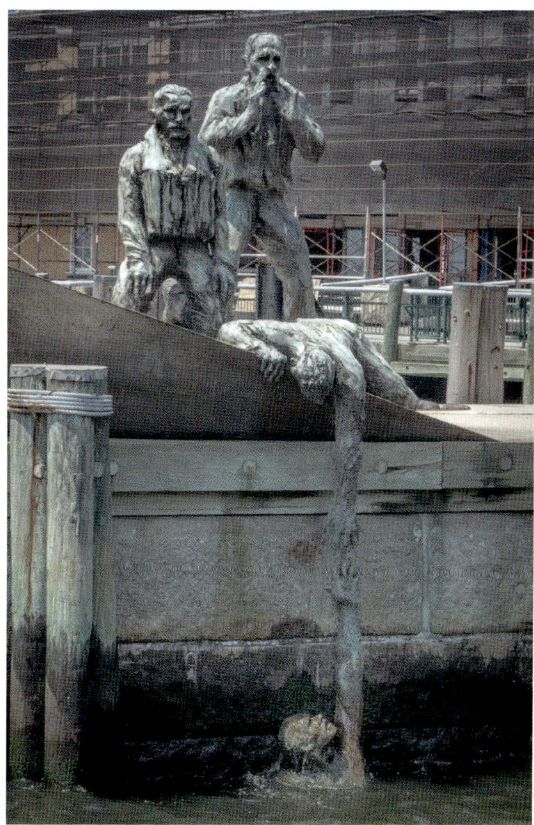

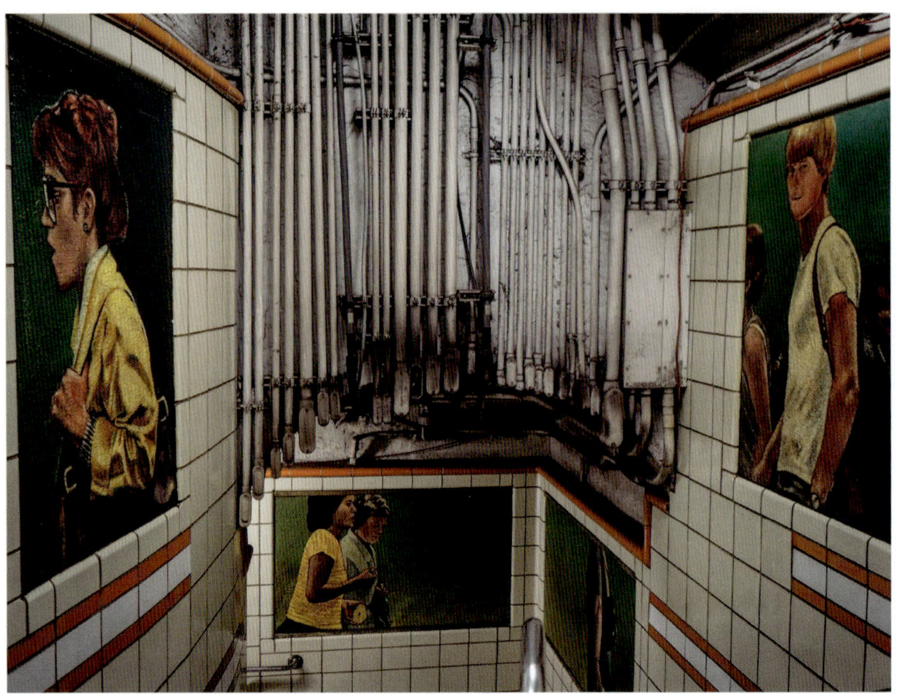

Art in the subway is juxtaposed against these gray pipes.

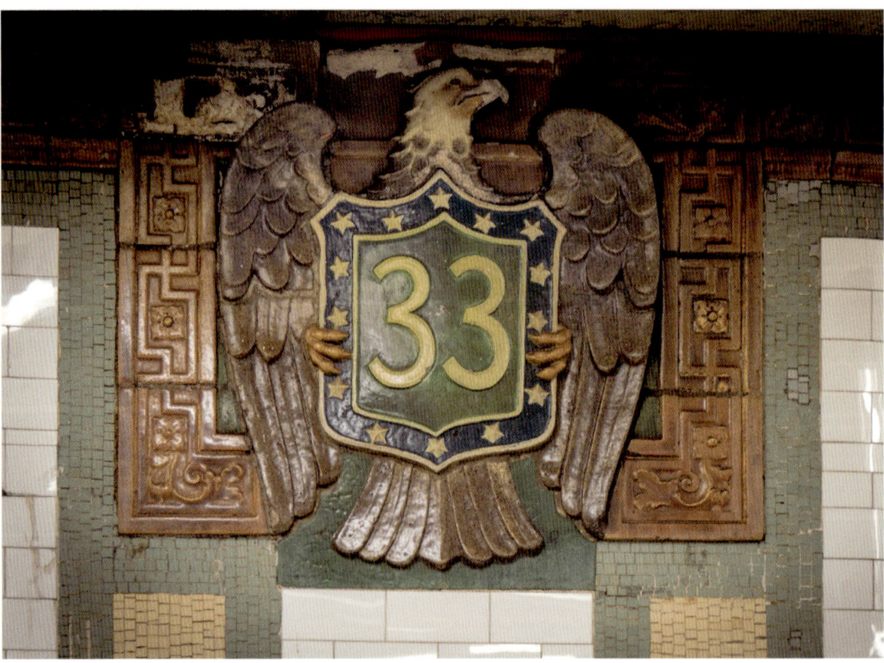

The 33rd Street subway station at Lexington St., built in 1904, is served by the 6 train. This station was originally part of the IRT (Interborough Rapid Transit Company line). New York once had three subway lines until they were all combined into the MTA (Metropolitan Transit Authority) in 1940. The IRT line hired architects Heins and LaFarge to beautify the stations; they designed these faience ceramics (pottery with a fine tin glaze) to adorn the stations.

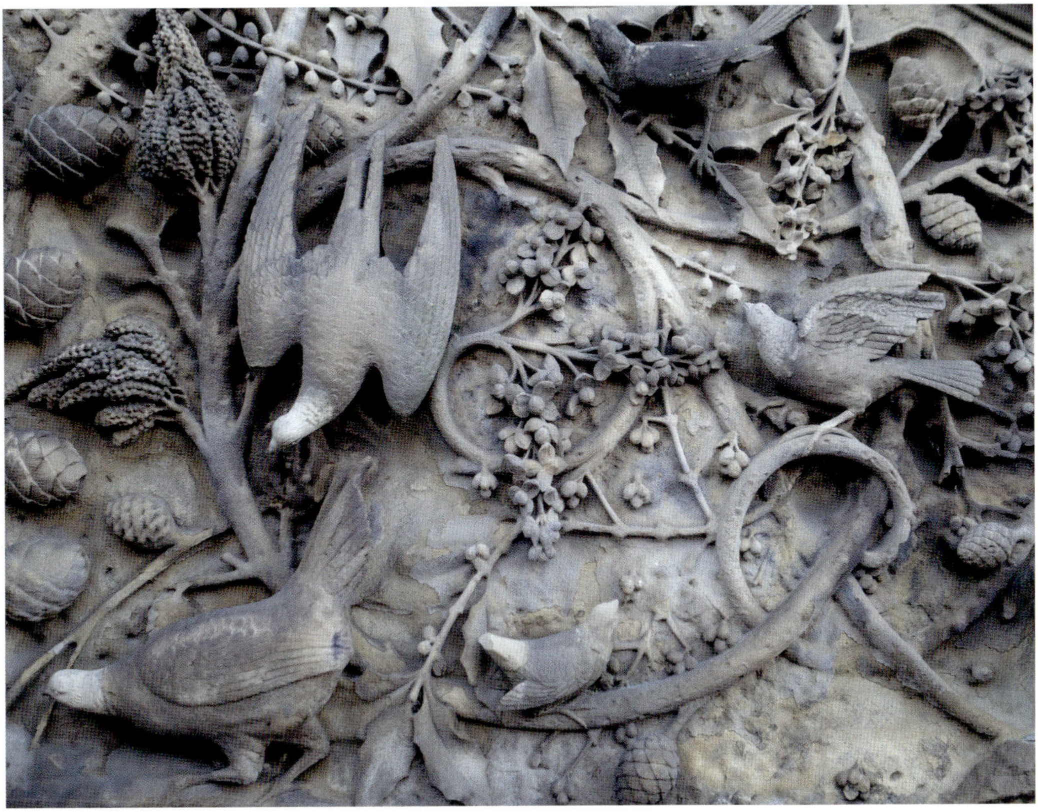

Detail from a sculpture in Central Park at the famous Bethesda Fountain.

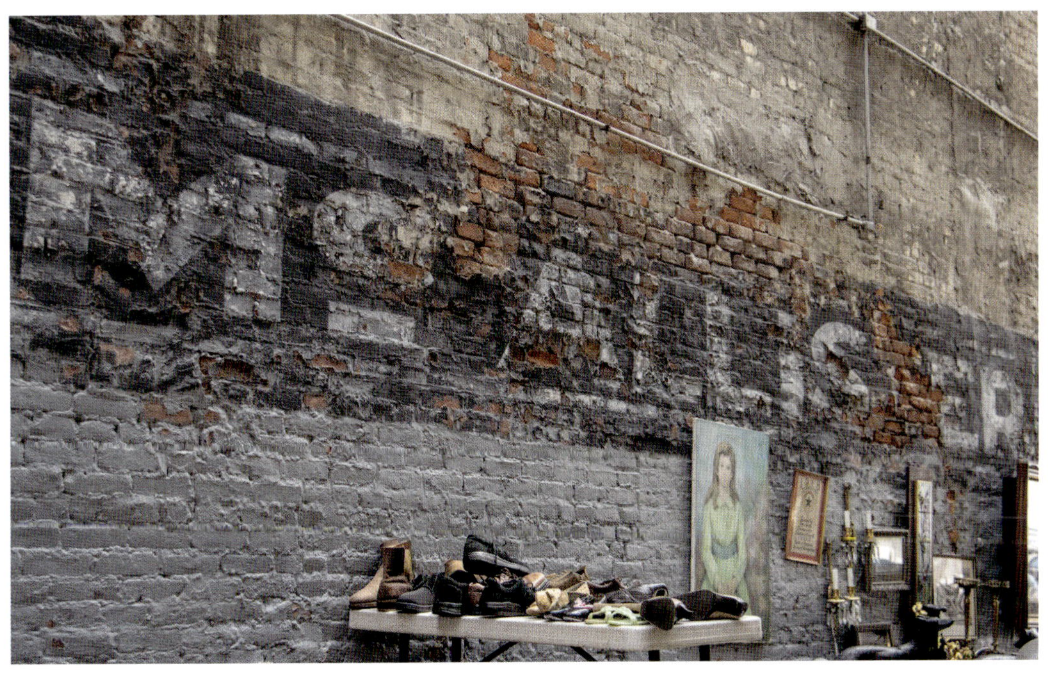

A faded ad can still be seen at a weekly flea market lot on 23rd Street.

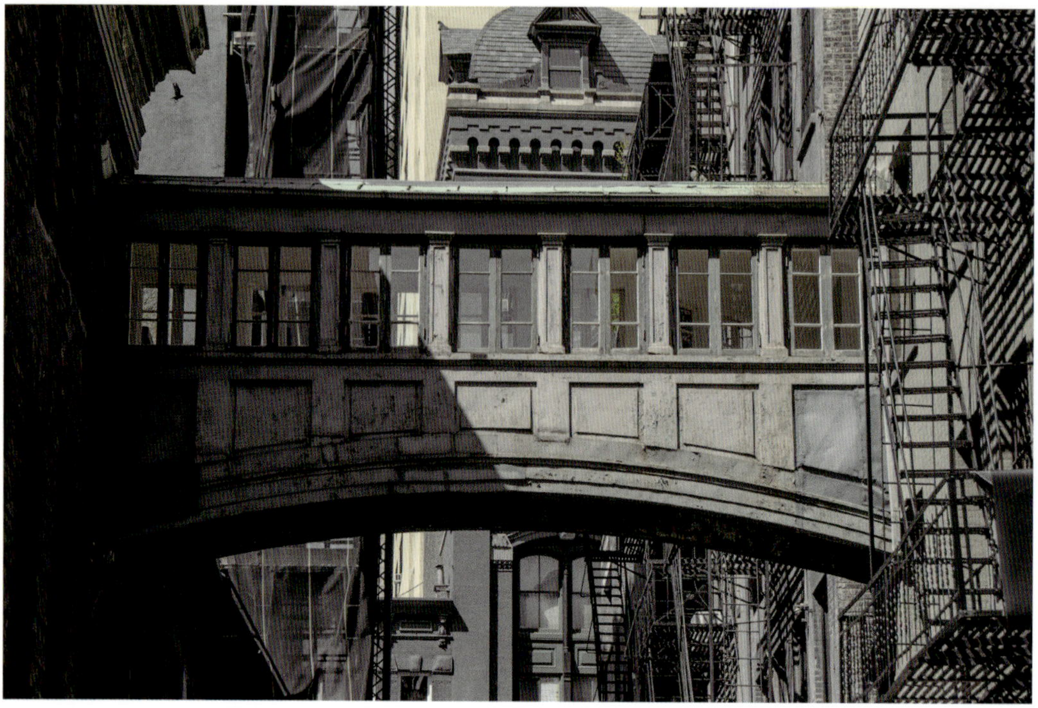

In Tribeca, one of the few remaining crosswalks between buildings is closed to the public.

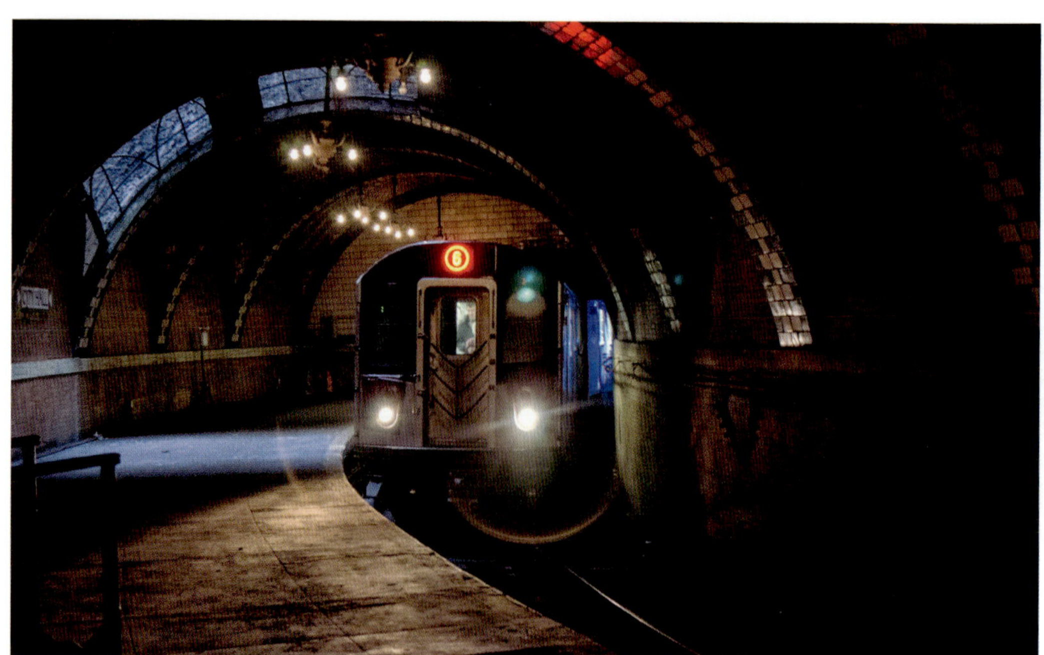

City Hall Subway Station was abandoned in 1945. This was the terminus of the IRT line when New York had competing subway lines. The station is on a curve, and as the trains got longer, there was a gap too large to accommodate the opening of the center door. Ridership had been declining as well, riders preferring the nearby Brooklyn Bridge station. City Hall Station is now used as a turnaround on the 6 line. Savvy riders may be able to get a glimpse of the station as the train makes its way back uptown.

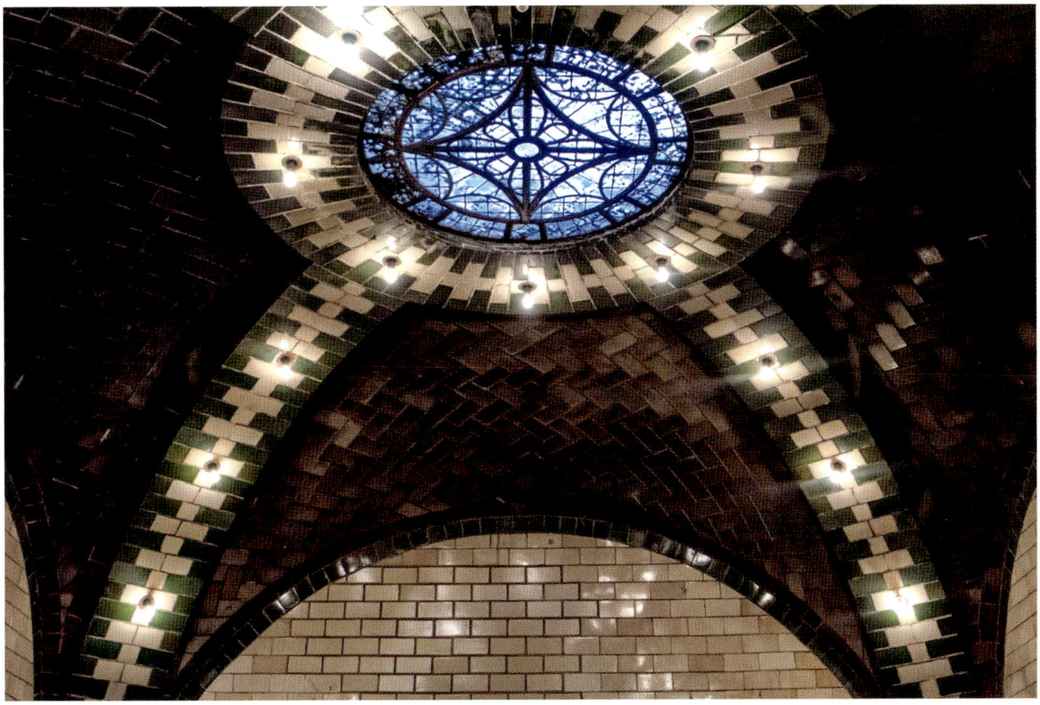

The City Hall Station, opened in 1904, is elaborately decorated with vaulted ceilings, skylights, glass tiles, and chandeliers.

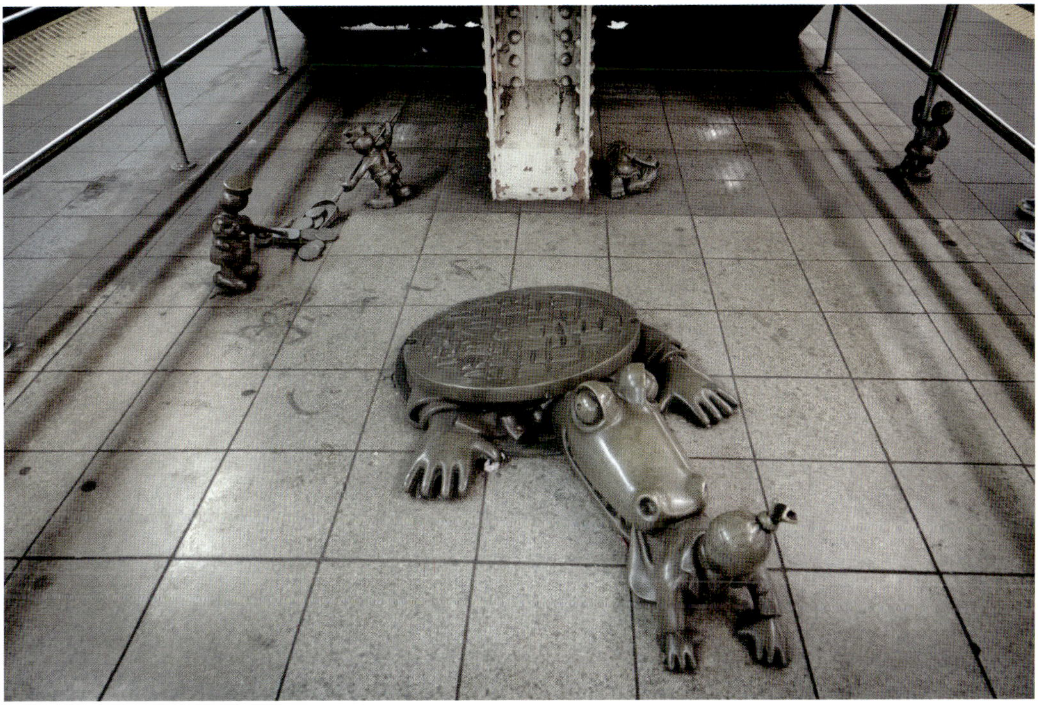

The MTA commissioned 170 of these whimsical statues by Tom Otterness for 14th Street subway station at 8th Ave. The cost of the statues was $200,000 in 2001.

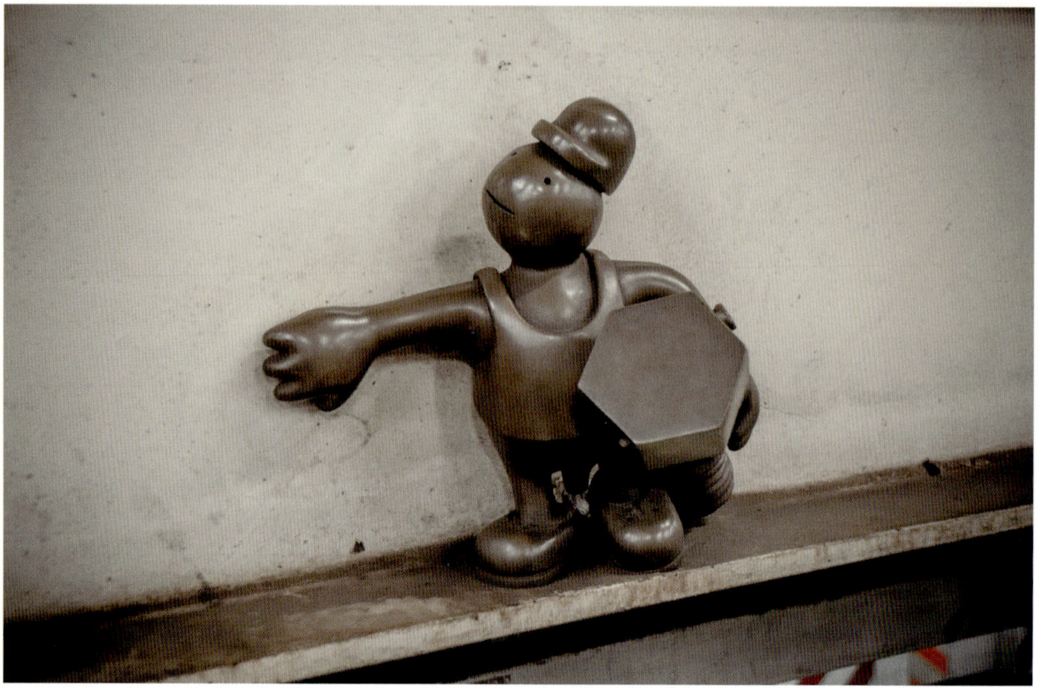

Called *Life Underground*, one of Otterness's inspirations was the political cartoonist Thomas Nast. Nast was famous for cartoons depicting the corruption of Tammany Hall, among other subjects, and these little creatures depict some of Nast's drawings.

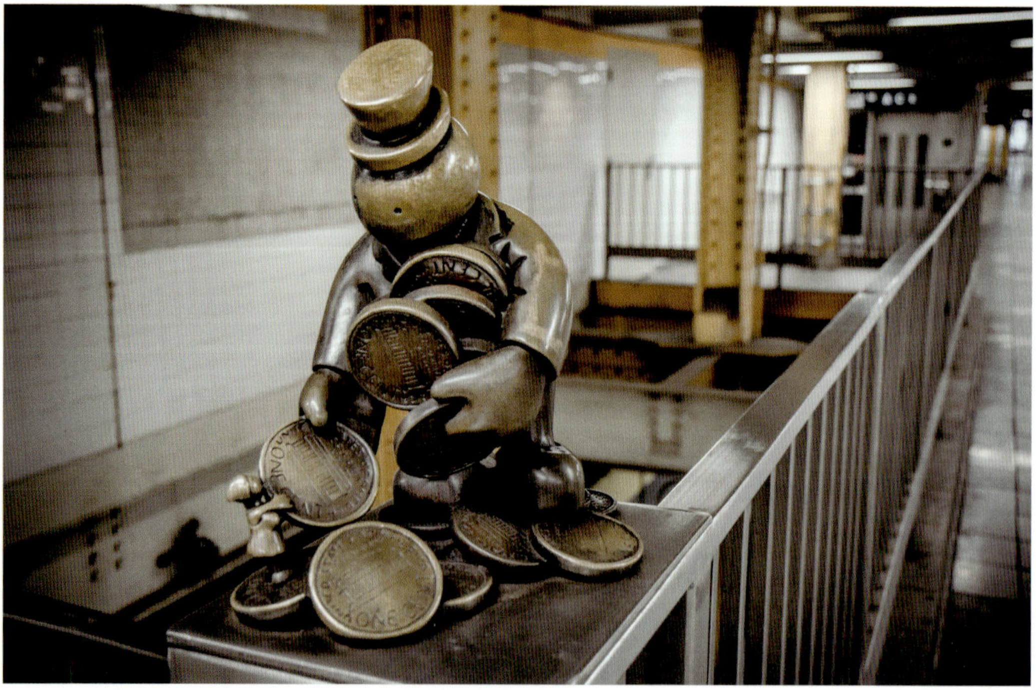

The main concept of these bronze statues was to portray class and money, or the lack thereof; this one depicts a man with money taking even more from a small child.

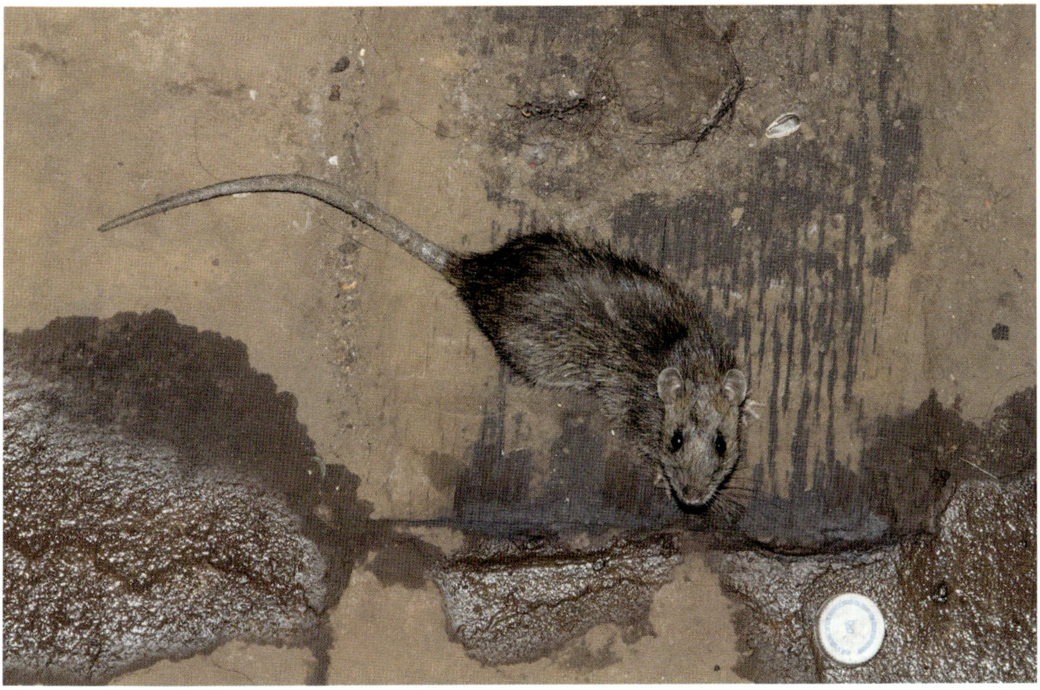

Above: Subway rat.

Right: The end of the road, Coney Island.

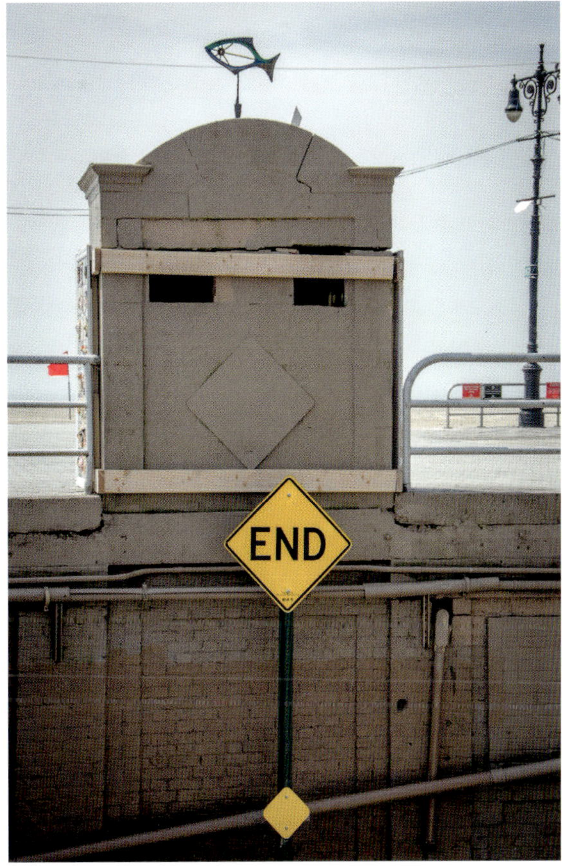

BIBLIOGRAPHY

"33rd STREET EAGLES." Forgotten New York, 21 July 2015, forgotten-ny.com/2015/07/33rd-street-eagles/.

"5 Beekman Street." Atlas Obscura, 17 Jan. 2012, www.atlasobscura.com/places/5-beekman-street.

Als, Hilton. "The Sugar Sphinx." *The New Yorker*, The New Yorker, 8 Sept. 2017, www.newyorker.com/culture/culture-desk/the-sugar-sphinx.

Balkrishna, Anna, and Erin O'Hara. "The Secrets of New York." NYCgo.com, NYC & Company, 16 Jan. 2019, www.nycgo.com/articles/new-york-secrets-slideshow.

"BAT: Brooklyn Army Terminal." BAT/Brooklyn Army Terminal, www.bklynarmyterminal.com/building-information/history/.

Blakinger, Keri. "The Story behind the Strange 8th Ave. Subway Statues and the Cartoons That Inspired Them ." Nydailynews.com, *New York Daily News*, 9 Apr. 2018, www.nydailynews.com/new-york/manhattan/story-behind-strange-8th-ave-subway-statues-article-1.2533216.

Bliss, Laura. "The High Line's Biggest Issue-And How Its Creators Are Learning From Their Mistakes." CityLab, 28 Feb. 2017, www.citylab.com/solutions/2017/02/the-high-lines-next-balancing-act-fair-and-affordable-development/515391/.

Bly, Nellie. *Ten Days in a Mad-House: or, Nellie Bly's Experience on Blackwell's Island: Feigning Insanity in Order to Reveal Asylum Horrors*. N.L. Munro, 1887.

Bredderman, Will. "Photo Exhibit Celebrates Coney's Iconic Countenance." *Brooklyn Paper*, 23 May 2014, www.brooklynpaper.com/photo-exhibit-celebrates-coneys-iconic-countenance-2/.

"Brooklyn Army Terminal." Brooklyn Relics, 20 Oct. 2013, brooklynrelics.blogspot.com/2013/10/brooklyn-army-terminal.html.

Brown, Samantha. "A $110 Million Castle in the Sky: Elegran's Real Estate Blog." New York Apartments & Condos for Sale & Rent/Elegran Real Estate, 4 June 2014, www.elegran.com/blog/2014/06/a-110-million-castle-in-the-sky.

Budds, Diana. "The Brooklyn Navy Yard Is Reinventing Architecture-and Itself." Curbed NY, 27 Sept. 2018, ny.curbed.com/2018/9/27/17906392/brooklyn-navy-yard-master-plan-wxy-vertical-manufacrturing.

"Building 92." Brooklyn Navy Yard, brooklynnavyyard.org/visit/bldg-92.

David, Joshua, and Robert Hammond. *High Line: The Inside Story of New York City's Park in the Sky*. Farrar, Straus and Giroux, 2013.

De Vries, Susan. "A Newly Rehabbed Roof Is Gleaming at the Historic Weir Greenhouse in Greenwood Heights." Brownstoner, 21 Nov. 2018, www.brownstoner.com/architecture/brooklyn-architecture-green-wood-weir-greenhouse-750-5th-avenue.

"Domino Park: Artifacts." Domino Park: Artifacts, www.dominopark.com/artifacts.

"Domino Park: History." Domino Park: History, www.dominopark.com/history.

"Doomed Merchant Mariners Memorial, New York, New York." RoadsideAmerica.com, www.roadsideamerica.com/story/23433.

"Doomed Merchant Mariners Memorial, New York, New York." RoadsideAmerica.com, www.roadsideamerica.com/story/23433.

"Ellis Island Closes." History.com, A&E Television Networks, 24 Nov. 2009, www.history.com/this-day-in-history/ellis-island-closes.

"ELLIS ISLAND NATIONAL MONUMENT." New York Architecture Images, www.nyc-architecture.com/LM/LM001-ELLISISLAND.htm.

"Ferry Building." Save Ellis Island, saveellisisland.org/rehab/ferry-building.

"Floyd Bennett Field." Forgotten New York, 19 Mar. 2012, forgotten-ny.com/2003/04/floyd-bennett-field/.

"Floyd Bennett Field." National Parks Service, U.S. Department of the Interior, www.nps.gov/gate/learn/historyculture/floyd-bennett-field.htm.

"Fort Tilden." National Parks Service, U.S. Department of the Interior, www.nps.gov/gate/learn/historyculture/fort-tilden.htm.

Geier, Stephanie. "The Top 10 Secrets of NYC's 5 Beekman Street, Formerly Temple St." Untapped New York, 8 Feb. 2019, untappedcities.com/2015/11/03/top-10-secrets-of-nycs-5-beekman-place-formerly-temple-court/.

Grundhauser, Eric. "Brooklyn Army Terminal Building B." Atlas Obscura, 13 Apr. 2015, www.atlasobscura.com/places/brooklyn-army-terminal-building-b.

Hagen, Ben. "Fort Tilden." Untapped New York, 15 Oct. 2016, untappedcities.com/2011/08/09/fort-tilden/.

"History If the Yard." Brooklyn Navy Yard, brooklynnavyyard.org/about/history.

History.com Editors. "Woolworth Building." History, A&E Television Networks, 22 Apr. 2010, www.history.com/topics/landmarks/woolworth-building.

"History: The Ruin." Friends of the Ruin, www.theruin.org/history-ruin.

"Hotel Rooms & Suites in NYC: The Beekman, a Thompson Hotel." Hotel Rooms & Suites in NYC | The Beekman, a Thompson Hotel, 30 Mar. 2020, www.thebeekman.com/rooms/.

Ingall, Marjorie. "Inside Ellis Island's Immigrant Hospital." Tablet, Morton Landowne, 10 Oct. 2017, www.tabletmag.com/jewish-life-and-religion/246347/inside-ellis-islands-immigrant-hospital.

Leon, Alexandra. "Brooklyn Navy Yard Rooted in History Long Before Clinton-Sanders Debate." DNAinfo New York, DNAinfo New York, 13 Apr. 2016, www.dnainfo.com/new-york/20160413/navy-yard/brooklyn-navy-yard-rooted-history-long-before-clinton-sanders-debate/.

"Life Underground Sculptures.", Atlas Obscura, 6 Jan. 2012, www.atlasobscura.com/places/life-underground.

McDonald, Martha. "Restoration of Childs' Restaurant in Coney Island." Traditional Building, 6 June 2018, www.traditionalbuilding.com/palladio-awards/childs-restaurant.

"McGovern Weir Greenhouse." Atlas Obscura, 29 Oct. 2013, www.atlasobscura.com/places/mcgovern-weir-greenhouse.

Pham, Diane. "Accounting for the Strange Faces That Adorn the Woolworth Building And

Other Fun Facts)." 6sqft, 23 Oct. 2014, www.6sqft.com/accounting-for-the-strange-faces-adorning-the-woolworth-building-and-other-fun-facts/.
Reeves, Pamela. *Ellis Island: Gateway to the American Dream*. Barnes & Noble Books, 2006.
Reid, Robert. "Best Things to Do on Roosevelt Island in New York City." Lonely Planet, 14 May 2019, www.lonelyplanet.com/articles/new-york-city-roosevelt-island.
Robledo, S. Jhoanna. "A Look Inside the Accidentally Preserved 5 Beekman Street." Intelligencer, 9 Sept. 2014, nymag.com/intelligencer/2014/09/look-inside-5-beekman-street-video.html.
"Roosevelt Island Smallpox Hospital Ruins." Atlas Obscura, 13 Jan. 2010, www.atlasobscura.com/places/roosevelt-island-smallpox-hospital-ruins.
Sawyer, Jonathan. "This Five-Story Penthouse Reigns Over Lower Manhattan." Highsnobiety, Open Menu All News Work from Home Style Sneakers Spring Sales Magazine Shop Search, 21 Sept. 2017, www.highsnobiety.com/2017/09/21/woolworth-pinnacle-penthouse/.
Senison, Heather. "Woolworth Penthouse Relisted For $79 Million, Showcases New Interior Renderings." *Forbes*, Forbes Magazine, 6 Nov. 2019, www.forbes.com/sites/heathersenison/2019/11/06/woolworth-building-penthouse-relisted-for-79-million-showcases-new-interior-renderings/#e6b171945203.
"The Ten Coolest Things at the Brooklyn Navy Yard." Brooklyn Eagle, 22 July 2015, brooklyneagle.com/articles/2015/07/22/the-ten-coolest-things-at-the-brooklyn-navy-yard/.
Welch, Adrian. "Queens Theatre in the Park - 1964 World's Fair Complex - e-Architect." e-Architect, 1 Oct. 2019, www.e-architect.co.uk/new-york/queens-theatre-worlds-fair.
"The Woolworth Building." Atlas Obscura, 13 Nov. 2014, www.atlasobscura.com/places/the-woolworth-building-new-york-new-york.
Xu, Susan. "The Top 10 Secrets of the Brooklyn Navy Yard." Untapped New York, 9 Mar. 2019, untappedcities.com/2016/12/16/top-10-secrets-of-the-brooklyn-navy-yard/.